IF CHRIST IS THE ANSWER

TOM SKINNER

WHAT ARE THE QUESTIONS ?

IF CHRIST IS THE ANSWER

TOM SKINNER

WHAT ARE THE QUESTIONS ?

ZONDERVAN PUBLISHING HOUSE

OF THE ZONDERVAN CORPORATION
GRAND RAPIDS, MICHIGAN 49506

IF CHRIST IS THE ANSWER,
WHAT ARE THE QUESTIONS?

Copyright © 1974 by Tom Skinner
Published by The Zondervan Corporation
Grand Rapids, Michigan

Library of Congress Catalog Card Number 73-22696

Quotations from the Bible are from the *King James Version; The New International Version, New Testament,* Copyright © 1973 by the New York Bible Society International, and published by The Zondervan Corporation; and *The Revised Standard Version,* New Testament Section, Second Edition, Copyright © 1972 by the Division of Christian Education of the National Council of Churches of Christ in the United States of America. Where no version is designated, the author has given a free translation.

Printed in the United States of America

To
Lauren Karmeel Skinner
my eldest daughter, whose love, compassion,
maturity, and understanding have been a tower
of strength to her father

CONTENTS

PREFACE

The story is told of a teenage boy who had just decided to give his life to Jesus Christ. He was instructed, "Now that you have become a Christian you must tell other people about Christ. You must find a way to witness about your faith." So the young man thought about the best method he could use to communicate Jesus Christ. He finally hit upon a scheme. He entered his classroom at school every morning about five minutes ahead of the rest of the class and wrote across the chalkboard in the front of the room in large bold letters CHRIST IS THE ANSWER. And then he would sit down very proudly as each of his classmates would file into the classroom and see this bold Christian witness on the chalkboard. Finally, one morning a sharp pagan kid came in right behind him and wrote under the bottom, CHRIST IS THE AN-SWER, *but what are the questions?*

For so long Christians have been hollering at people CHRIST IS THE ANSWER without a serious consideration as to what the problem is. I can hear my Algebra teacher, when I was in the eighth grade, drilling in our heads over and over again: "In order to solve an algebraic problem you must define the problem before you come up with a solution. Define the problem before the solution."

I do not believe that in our generation Christians have

clearly defined the problem. Back in the late '30s and early '40s when our country was experiencing a wave of revivalism, our parents and grandparents who were in the middle of that revival always answered any question by saying, CHRIST IS THE ANSWER. If you said there is a war going on, they said, "Christ is the answer." If you said black people are being lynched, there's a race problem in America, they said, "Christ is the answer." The water and the air are being polluted; they said, "Christ is the answer." Today their children and their grandchildren are caught up in a wave of Jesus Movements across the country and if you say to these kids that there's a race problem in America, they say, "One way." There's an air pollution problem; they say, "One way." There's a war problem; they say, "One way." Like their parents, they have refused to face up to the problem.

For the last ten years I have been preaching and teaching on the major university, college, and high school campuses of this country, and non-Christian young people keep asking the major questions. And I have found through that ministry that you cannot escape those questions by simply saying, "Christ is the answer." We must deal with the question. I attended a Jesus Rally not long ago in which there was a testimony meeting. Various people would get up and explain what Jesus Christ meant to them. Several young people's testimonies went like this, "We used to be involved in the cities in trying to get better housing for people, trying to get people to vote, trying to get food and clothing and a better way of life for poor people. But now that we've come to know Jesus Christ we don't have to be involved in any of that anymore." I must confess to you that I was sick to my stomach. Because there is the kind of evangelism in this country which is insisting that we can whitewash the problems and the questions simply by telling people that Christ is the answer.

I must confess to you also that writing this book and taking this position puts me in a strange dilemma because I am an evangelist. That means I have been given the gift to communicate the message of Jesus Christ in such a way as to persuade people that Jesus Christ is where it's at. In that sense I would be labeled an evangelical or a salvationist. On the other hand, I believe that those people who are committed to the kingdom of God have to lay their bodies on the line and meet the needs of the total man. There's no sense in preaching "Jesus saves" to a man whose stomach is growling so loud that he can't hear what you're saying. So man has to be fed physically, emotionally, mentally as well as spiritually. That would also label me a social activist.

I have been reluctant to write this book. In fact, I have been advised by some people who have read the manuscript not to have it published. Much of this is due to what I call the economics of evangelism. I'm president of Tom Skinner Associates, which is made up of men and women who are committed to communicating the message of Jesus Christ and all of its ramifications to everybody in general and black people in particular. The institutions we want to address ourselves to in our society, and where the need is the greatest, are controlled by the social activists. These people will be very disturbed about what they would call my simplistic position in seeking to call people to a personal relationship with Jesus Christ. Yet the people who support an evangelical message are the salvationists who will have some tremendous problems with my social activism. I get it from both sides. So I've decided to practice what I preach — believe God, speak the truth, and let the chips fall where they may.

Well, let's get on with it — what are the questions?

THE WILL OF GOD

How can I know the will of God? How do I know if God is asking me to do something, or if what I want to do is my own thing?

NINETY-NINE point nine percent of the will of God is written in the Word of God. Therefore, if one really wants to know what God is about, what God is requiring of him, he must search the Scriptures. He must know the Word of God. Many people try to arrive at the will of God through mental gymnastics or through trying to properly interpret their circumstances. Another group of people, when they think of the will of God, tend to think of it in terms of vocation. Most people who ask the question "What is the will of God?" are essentially talking about "What job does God want me to have? What kind of vocation does He want me to go into? What does God want me to do when I graduate from school?" Really, all that has nothing to do with the will of God.

For instance, if you read Romans 8:28, 29, you have a clear outline of the will of God. First, the will of God is that everything in your life works together for God's good. In other words, you exist for God's good, and if you're committed to Jesus Christ, you want what is good for Him. Now, whatever in your life works out for God's good will work out for your good because your good is God's good.

The second thing in the will of God is that you love Him above every other love in your life. Third, that you allow Him from day to day to conform you to His image, so that each day you become more and more like Jesus in terms of your attitude, behavior, and lifestyle. Finally, you become the link in God's chain of introducing other people to Jesus Christ. That is the will of God. Whether you end up working for

General Motors or IBM or rowing a boat on the Amazon River is incidental.

This is why the Apostle Paul exhorted his protégé, Timothy, "Study to show yourself approved unto God, a servant who does not need to be embarrassed, rightly dividing the Word of Truth" (2 Tim. 2:15). What he was talking about was the study of God's point of view, which comes from the Scriptures. The other reason for studying the Scriptures is that it is the only way you can deal with sin. For that reason the psalmist said, "Your word have I hid in my heart that I might not sin against you" (Ps. 119:11). It is very interesting that in each of the three times Jesus Christ was tempted by the devil in the wilderness, He responded by saying, "It is written, . . . It is written, . . . It is written, ..." The only way to deal with temptation and the possible alienation of your life from God is to know what God is saying to you, and that comes clearly through His Word.

God has married the Word of God and the Holy Spirit together. You cannot have one without the other. If you attempt to have the Word of God without the Holy Spirit, you are left with cold, dead legalism — a lot of rules and regulations — but if you attempt to have the Holy Spirit without the Word of God, you end up with emotionalism and extremism. You must have the Word of God and the Holy Spirit together to properly interpret the will of God through your circumstances.

The tragedy of those people who are constantly looking at the will of God in terms of vocation is that they are always thinking about the future and never think in terms of the will of God today. A college freshman comes to me and says, "Tom, I want you to pray for me that I might know the will of God." And of course, he is trying to find out the will of God in terms of what he is supposed to do when he graduates. In his sophomore year he comes back to me and says, "Pray for me. I'm trying to know the will of God." In his junior year he says, "Pray for me. I want to know the will of God." In his senior year he is saying, "Pray for me. I want to know the will of God." The day after he graduates from school, he is run over by a car and killed...so he has missed four years of the will of God in looking for it. You see, the will of God is not down the road; it is today, right at this moment.

A classic illustration of this is the young man who is told by his father to deliver a package to some friends about ten miles along the road. The young fellow gets into the car and pulls out of the driveway; thirty seconds later he pulls back into the driveway and comes into the house. "What's wrong?" his father asks. "Why haven't you gone?" The boy answers, "Can't drive, dad! There's a heavy fog outside and I can't see." His father says, "Son, how far can you see?" He answers, "I can see twenty-five feet, that's all. The fog is so thick, the farthest I can see in front of the car is twenty-five feet." So his dad says, "Well, get in the car and drive twenty-five feet." The idea is that if you drive twenty-five feet, then you will see another twenty-five feet.

Now, in terms of the will of God, you may not see clearly all the way down the road, but you take the step toward what you can see. If you can see only five feet in front of you, then walk the five feet and you will see another five. The will of God does not have to be totally explained to you as to what is going to happen to you from now until the day you die. You just take one step at a time on the basis of what you know from Scripture, your circumstances, and other truth God has given.

What is the real purpose for my life?

I BELIEVE the purpose of God for your life and mine is summed up in Romans 8:28 in the New Testament. It goes like this: "We know that in all things God works for the good of those who love him, who have been called according to his purpose" (NIV). Verse 29 says, "For whom He did know in advance He did also determine to be conformed to the image of His Son, that He might be the firstborn among many brothers."

First of all, the purpose of God is that everything in your life work together for God's good. Often this might be at your inconvenience. If you really love God, you will want what is good for God; and when everything in your life is working out for God's good, then it is working out for your good, because your good is God's good. All things work together for the good to them who love God.

The second purpose of God is that you love Him above every other love in your life. You read, for instance, in Luke 14:26 that Jesus Christ says, "If any man would come after me and does not hate mother, father, sister, brother, husband, wife, children, and his own life also, he cannot be my disciple."

By this Jesus does not mean we are to hate our loved ones with literal hatred, but He does mean our love for Him should supersede every other love in our lives. Unfortunately, there is a group of people in this country known as the "Children of God" who advocate that we should forsake our husbands, wives, mothers, and fathers in the name of Jesus. This is not what the Bible is saying. It is saying that if there is a showdown between what Christ wants and what your parents want; what Christ wants and what your husband wants; what Christ wants and what your children want; what Christ wants and what your sister and brother want — Jesus Christ gets first place. But He does call us to honor and to be committed to these loved ones in such a way that our love for Him will supersede every other love in our lives. That is God's purpose.

Then His purpose is to conform you to the image of His Son. This will happen through your commitment to Him and in allowing the resurrected Christ to live His life out through the common clay of your humanity. Your humanity becomes a vehicle through which Jesus Christ expresses Himself. As you allow this to happen, as you study the Word of God, read what God is saying to you, and then walk in obedience to His Word by asking His spirit to help you obey Him, each day

The Will of God

you will become more and more like Jesus in your character and disposition.

Finally, it says this is all done so Jesus Christ might be the firstborn among many brothers. This seems like a contradiction because all the way through the Bible it says, "For God so loved the world that he gave his one and only Son" (John 3:16 NIV). John 1:14 says, "We have seen his glory, the glory of the one and only Son, who came from the Father" (NIV). In Romans 8:29 it says He is not the only begotten anymore — He is the firstborn. The question is, How did Jesus Christ change from the only begotten to the firstborn? It is simple: I'm the oldest in my family. I come from a family of four boys and one girl. Now, for the first two years of my life I was my parents' one and only son. Whenever guests came to our home, or whenever we went somewhere, they always put me on display as being their only son Tom. Two years after my birth my brother was born, and it took some of the limelight away. But when my brother was born, I ceased to be my parents' one and only son and I became their eldest or their firstborn. With every son or daughter my parents had after that, I became the eldest of that many more brothers and sisters.

God, like any normal father, wanted to have more children. The whole purpose of God is to take His Son Jesus Christ out of the realm of being the only begotten and to make Him the firstborn by having more children, to expand the family of God. God's purpose is to use you to be the vehicle through which He expresses Himself both in lifestyle and verbal communication to confront other people with His claims. People will see Christ in you, hear the Gospel from you, and invite Jesus Christ to be Lord of their lives. Thus the kingdom of God will continue to expand, and Jesus will become the eldest of that many more brothers and sisters.

That's God's purpose: (1) you love Him above every other love in your life; (2) everything in your life will work together for God's good, no matter how inconvenient it seems for you; (3) every day you become more and more like Him, allowing Him to live His life out through you; and (4) finally you become the link in God's chain in introducing other people to Jesus Christ so that He becomes the eldest brother among a large family of people who are trusting Him. Where you do that, how you do it, whether you do it as a pastor, evangelist, doctor, lawyer, garbage collector, taxicab driver, truck driver, housewife, singer, or entertainer, is irrelevant as long as you do it.

As I read your book Black and Free *and the story of your life as a gang leader on the streets of Harlem, then your encounter with Jesus Christ, it was obvious you made a 180-degree turn. But what does that do for those who do not feel the need for this kind of change?*

FIRST OF ALL, many persons are confused about the whole question of sin and the need for change. Most of us, when we define "sinners," define them as thieves, drug addicts, alcoholics, murderers, prostitutes, etc. And many people who are more middle class in their values tend to look upon these other people as sinners and upon themselves as fairly moral representatives of society. But God doesn't put sin into categories. Sin is separation from God. Sin is man doing his own thing instead of God's thing, which is why the prophet Isaiah says, "Let the wicked forsake his way...and let him return unto the Lord" (55:7 kjv). So it is possible to be very moral and very righteous, according to the standards of morality of the society, and yet be a sinner because one is running his own life. Sin is being devoid of the life of God. That is why Jesus Christ came into the world for the purpose of reconciling men to God.

It is easy to look at my kind of background as a gang leader —putting knives in people's bodies—and say, "Well, it was good for Tom Skinner to be converted because he was bad,

20

but I don't need that kind of conversion because I'm not a bad person." But you have to understand "bad" as determined by God. I was quite content as a gang leader, I had power and 129 fellows following me, eating out of my hand, doing whatever I asked them. I was content in that position of popularity and power. But I discovered through the presentation of the gospel of Jesus Christ to me that what made me a sinner was that my entire lifestyle was doing my thing instead of God's thing.

Every human being who does not have the life of God in him needs this 180-degree turn. The Bible says, "All have sinned and come short of the standards of God, . . . there is none righteous, no not one" (Rom. 3:23; 3:10). Again, the Bible says, "All our righteousnesses are as filthy rags" (Isa. 64:6 KJV), which means that man at his best comes out nothing more than a dirty rag according to the standards of God. Therefore, all people need this type of conversion.

The other thing to keep in mind is that the manifestation of sin will be determined by one's environment, but the *fact* of sin is *not* determined by the environment. In other words, I will sin no matter what kind of environment I live in. My environment simply determines the way in which I will sin. If I were a thief in Harlem, where I was born and raised, I would have to raid people's apartments, jump people on the streets, snatch people's pocketbooks, hold up or rob stores, and rob people on elevators. But if I were a businessman living in a suburban community, I would not steal that way; I would steal by padding my business account, cheating on my income taxes, taking kickbacks in my business, promising promotions to people if they extended the kind of money and favors to me. In other words, one's environment determines how one sins, but sin *will* be manifested in one form or another. Therefore, we must not judge the outworking of sin because it will change, depending on the geographic location in which one lives.

What caused you to change your way of living?

FOR SEVERAL years I was a gang leader on the streets of Harlem, leading a group known as the Harlem Lords in rioting, looting, stealing—a generally violent kind of life. I was mapping out strategy for a gang fight one night which was to be the largest gang fight ever to take place in New York City. It would have involved five gangs. If I were to succeed in leading the fellows to victory in this particular fight, I would emerge as the leader of an alliance of gangs that would make me the most powerful leader in the area. I had my radio on that night, listening to my favorite disc jockey, which was a rock and roll program that came on every night between the hours of eight and ten o'clock. Normally at nine o'clock there is a station break, a commercial, and the deejay should return to the air with the rest of the program.

On this particular night, instead of the deejay returning to the air after the station break and the commercial, an unscheduled program came on and a man began to speak from 2 Corinthians 5:17. That verse says, "Therefore, if anyone is in Christ, he is a new creation; the old has gone, the new has come!" (NIV). He went on to say that every person born into the human race was born without the life of God and that it is the absence of God's life that causes a person to be what the Bible calls a sinner. He went on to tell me that Jesus Christ was the only person who ever lived who was both the truth about God and the truth about man. Christ was the only man who ever lived the way God intended man to live. I could never be what God intended me to be without inviting this Christ—who died on the cross because He was capable of forgiving me of my sins, and who rose again from the dead — to live in me. Apart from Him I could never become a new person.

It was that simple message — that Christ died in my place and rose again to live in me — and my believing it, trusting it, and inviting Christ to live in my life that's changed my entire lifestyle. Keep in mind, though, that I didn't come to Jesus Christ simply because I was a gang leader. I came to Jesus Christ because I was in need of Him and in order to be a whole person.

Do you believe the Christian religion is a superior religion?

THE ANSWER to this question is No. When you are stacking religions up next to each other, any one of them can be superior, based upon what the particular need of the individual is. Religion is defined as what a person feels to be of ultimate value and the actions he takes in the light of it; so a person can be a Communist, a Buddhist, a Hindu, a Methodist, a Baptist, a Presbyterian, an agnostic or an atheist and be religious. If you put Christianity next to Buddhism or Hinduism, or Islam, it is quite possible that one of those religions is superior to Christianity in some ways. That is why I don't get involved in hassles over religion. Now, if you want to take the personalities around which those religions should be built and deal solely with the persons, you have a new ball game. If you want to stack Jesus Christ up next to Mohammed, or next to Confucius, you have a new ball game, because all those fellows are dead, but Jesus Christ is alive. That is why I would not cross the street to get a person interested in religion. Nor would I cross the street to get him interested in an institutional church. However, I would walk around the world to get people interested in Jesus Christ because He is where it's at. He is the only person who is alive from the dead and is prepared to live His life through every person who dares to trust Him.

You stated that since the time of your conversion you have not needed to "work" at being a Christian. I can't quite understand how you can say that. The Apostle Paul claims he had to work, and work hard. You yourself quote Romans 7, and you seem to be contradicting yourself. Could you explain your statement?

THE WORD "Christian" is divided into two parts, "Christ" — CHRIST, "ian" — IAN. That is Christ in you living His own life through you without any help or assistance from you. That is clear all the way through Scripture. The Apostle Paul says, "Christ in you, the hope of glory" (Col. 1:27 NIV). In Philippians 1:6 he says, "He who began a good work in you will carry it on to completion until the day of Christ Jesus," and then he says in 1 Thessalonians 5:24, "The one who calls you is faithful and he will do it" (NIV). For everything that Jesus calls you to do, He will turn around and do it in you as you make yourself available to Him. What you have to do is cooperate with Him.

Paul does talk about the struggle between the flesh and the spirit. But it is a struggle between God's Spirit and the self life. The answer is given to us when the Word of God says, "Walk in the Spirit, and you will not fulfill the lust of the flesh" (Gal. 5:16). The struggle comes when Satan turns that phrase back to front and says, "Don't fulfill the lusts of the flesh...stay away from that, don't touch that, don't go near that, and for God's sake don't look at that. There might come the glorious day when you walk in the Spirit."

It becomes difficult to live the Christian life when I spend all my time trying to overcome the sins in my life, hoping

The Will of God

that the more sins I overcome, the better I will be able to walk in the Spirit. But Scripture has it the other way around: "Live by the Spirit, and you will not gratify the desires of your sinful nature" (NIV). In Romans 7 Paul talks about the struggle of a man who wants to produce the Christian life apart from Jesus Christ. Paul says, "That which I would do, I do not do...that which I would not do, I do. I find another law that when I would do good, evil is present with me" (vv. 19, 21). He says, "What a messed-up man I am. Who will deliver me from the body of this death?" (v. 24). This is his struggle. Then he cites the answer to his struggle: I thank God through Jesus Christ that while my self life (my flesh) is out to serve the law of sin, the Spirit of Christ is in me, which has made me a new creation (cf. v. 25). Paul is going to serve the Lord, is going to walk in the Spirit. That is why Paul says in Romans 6:11, "Reckon yourselves to be dead unto sin and alive unto God." So my self life wants to serve sin, my self life wants to have its own way, but I'm not serving my self life. I starve my self life daily, by walking in the Spirit. It doesn't mean I am perfect, but I don't sit down and get hangups about my imperfections. I accept the fact that the blood of Jesus Christ cleanses me from all sin, that my self life was put to death on the cross, and I walk in the Spirit and accept that my self life is dead unto sin and my Spirit is alive unto God.

The other point is, I never said I learned this immediately after being converted. I went through the phase most Christians go through of trying to live up to a bunch of rules and regulations, trying very hard to be pious and holy and righteous and wear an adjusted halo over my head, saying the right evangelical Christian phrases, and being able to recite the right words and vocabulary. Until one day I discovered that 1,900 years ago, when Jesus Christ was nailed to the cross, I was nailed to the cross. That's why I don't have to go out and try to crucify myself, but count myself to be crucified. Christ has arisen from the dead to live His life in me. I don't have to make any effort to get Him to live in me. I have eternal life that nobody can take away, and I've learned to relax.

I do think much of this misunderstanding could be avoided in the lives of many Christians if those of us who preach evangelistically, those of us who communicate faith in Christ to people who do not know Him, were more accurate in our preaching. Most of our preaching says, "Just accept Jesus Christ as your personal Savior." Which means to offer a person a passport out of hell to heaven. But if you read the Scripture, you will see that at no time did the early disciples ever preach accepting Jesus Christ as "personal Savior." The early disciples said, "If you confess with your mouth, 'Jesus is Lord,' and believe in your heart that God raised him from the dead, you will be saved" (Rom. 10:9 NIV). The early disciples preached the lordship of Jesus as their salvation message: complete surrender, abandonment to His lordship. What we have today is a kind of cheap Gospel which says Accept Jesus as your personal Savior so you won't burn in hell, and a number of people have invited Jesus Christ into their lives simply to collect fire insurance. Then they have to struggle through many years of their Christian lives to make Him Lord, or go to Deeper Life Conferences where they learn how to make Him Lord. They could have avoided all that struggle if they had heard a more mature, holistic Gospel by which they could have been liberated into His lordship from the very beginning.

KEEPING SPIRITUALLY ALIVE

Our *pastor once gave the idea it is hard to keep spiritually alive without witnessing. Please give your comments on this.*

I THINK I understand what your pastor is saying. But I wouldn't say it that way. You do not witness to keep spiritually alive; instead, you witness because you *are* spiritually alive. In other words, it is through being spiritually alive that you will witness. It is what David is talking about when he says, "My cup runs over." Because of your worship, and because of the time you spend with God and the time you spend in His Word and the time you spend with others of God's people, your cup runs over — and what runs over spills out into the world, and that becomes your witness. In fact, in the Book of Acts (and throughout the New Testament for that matter) almost every time the Scripture says of Christians "and they were filled with the Holy Spirit," there always follows the statement that they spoke for Jesus. (See, for example, Acts 2; 4:8; 6:10; 7:55; 9:17-20; 19:6.) Speaking for Jesus always follows being filled with the Holy Spirit.

There are many people who say they are retiring and shy and all that kind of thing, but there is nothing about your nature or mine, whether aggressive, shy, or retiring, that ever exonerates us from being bold for Jesus. Witnessing is a result of being filled with the Holy Spirit. You do not witness in order to be filled with the Holy Spirit. When you are filled with the Holy Spirit, then a result of it will be that you witness. I think the point your pastor was trying to make is that there are a whole lot of people who claim to be filled with the Holy Spirit, but who do not confront other people with Jesus Christ. To that point he is right. A person who is not witnessing must not be filled with the Spirit. But there are many people who are witnessing who are not filled with the Spirit. You must be filled with the Holy Spirit, and then you will witness.

What method of evangelism do you find works best with teenagers?

THERE IS no one method of evangelism that works best with everybody. We must all have different tools, and as many different tools as possible, to communicate with as many different people as possible. Teenagers range in age from thirteen to nineteen, which makes them different from one another. Teenagers vary in educational background, which makes them different. In other words, you've got to use whatever tool communicates with the particular person you are dealing with. It is like playing golf. Most golfers carry something like eleven or twelve clubs in their bags, and each club has to be used dependent on where the ball is lying and how far the ball is from the green. When I'm on the green, I use a putter because I will be somewhere from one foot to forty feet away from the hole. But when I am 360 yards away, I use a driver. When the ball is in a sandtrap, I don't use a driver — I use a wedge. You use the club suitable to where the ball is lying. So you must carry in your bag of methods and techniques as many different tools as you can possibly come up with, and use the tool that is most appropriate for the person you are communicating with.

How do the hippies accept the Gospel?

IN THE 1970s we're going to see less and less of what has

been known as "the hippies," but in terms of their acceptance of the Gospel, it's been outstanding. Much of the Jesus Movement among a great number of young people in American society has involved hippies, "flower children," and drug-scene people. Many persons who five years ago were known as hippies are committed to Jesus Christ, to His lordship and authority, today. Not because living the hippie life was wrong but because they discovered vital living in Jesus Christ. It doesn't necessarily mean they've changed their lifestyle and started wearing ties and jackets and cutting their beards and shortening their hair, because short hair, tie, jacket, and conservative looks have absolutely nothing to do with being Christian. I've discovered it is far easier to engage in relevant conversation with the hippie-type kids concerning Jesus Christ than almost any other group of people in our society.

There are many people holding to the Christian faith who believe they should go into all the world and baptize people and thus make them Christians. Is that your bag?

NOT QUITE. When the Bible says, "Go and make disciples of all nations, baptizing them in the name of the Father and of the Son and of the Holy Spirit" (Matt. 28:19 NIV), the word "baptism" means to be "identified with." Jesus Christ was saying we are to go into all the world, confront people with the truth about Jesus Christ, and help them to become disciples. "Baptism" is a means of helping them to become identified with Him.

Water baptism is symbolic of the death and resurrection of Jesus Christ. When I go down into the water, I am saying that I am being buried with Him, which is symbolic of my self life, which has lived independent from God, being buried with Christ by baptism. Coming up out of the water speaks of the resurrection of Jesus. He arose from the dead as the leader of a new creation. Coming up out of the water indicates I've come up to begin a new life centered in Jesus Christ. You do not have to be baptized in order to become a Christian, that is, to have Christ come to reside in you. You are baptized in obedience to Christ and as an outward confession of an inward conviction.

At that point, neither I nor anyone else can make people become Christians. My job is that of an evangelist, and the word "evangelist" means "teller of good news." My job is to do nothing more than to confront people with the truth of Jesus Christ, exposing them to the validity of His claims, reasoning with them as to why He alone is able to put their lives together. The decision to trust Jesus Christ has to be left to the person whom I confront with this truth.

How old are you, and what made you become a minister?

I WAS BORN June 6, 1942. I decided to become a minister because that is what God calls everyone who has committed himself to Jesus Christ to be. We are all to be ministers. It is just that many of us play different roles within the confines of that word called "the ministry." My role happens to be an evangelist, which is a person who goes from place to place expounding the truth about Jesus Christ and calling men to Him. Another man will have the role of being a pastor, which means that he equips those people who are called of Jesus Christ for the work of the ministry. The reason I go from place to place to preach the gospel of Jesus Christ is just simply because God has told me to.

Is dancing all right?

I'M ASSUMING that you're asking, "Is it all right for a Christian to dance?" That question can only be answered between you and God personally. There are all kinds of evidence in Holy Scripture of dancing that occurred among the Hebrews. The Bible says, "David danced in the presence of God with all his might" (2 Sam. 6:14)`. Dancing has widely different objectives to different people. For some people it is a matter of grace, an art form, a creative expression. To other people it is a form of exercise. Still others see it as a form of entertainment.

Dancing is an issue that a great number of black people get frustrated over who attend predominantly white Christian college campuses, where dancing is discouraged. I've yet to find people who come up with valid arguments against it. Generally their arguments go: "I'm opposed to dancing because of what it will lead to." I don't know about you, but in my community people who want to go to bed with each other don't need to dance first. They don't need to dance to get ready.

Then there's the argument that dancing leads to sexual lust. Well, the problem is that dancing is far less sexually stimulating today because most people don't touch. The young people don't touch when they dance; they get out in the middle of the floor and get lost. It seems there was something far more enticing about the waltz and some of those old-time dances my mother and grandmother used to do than what the kids are doing today. Then there are those Christian colleges in the country which require that their students sign pledge cards on which they promise they will not dance while they are at school. I have a real problem with this, and for a number of reasons. Such colleges in the country have given the impression that dancing is wrong, and spiritually bad; many college administrators and trustees believe dancing is sinful. But not all of them. The truth of the matter is that we ought to start being honest with our young people about dancing. Few people have been able to come up with a sound biblical reason for not dancing.

It seems to me that at the Christian college and Christian institutional level, what we really want to say to our kids in an evangelical context is, "For every $1 we spend in tuition, the college has to raise $3 to keep you in school. This money must be raised from a group of people known as The Constituency — the donors, the checkwriters. The majority of the people who contribute to evangelical educational institutions are between the ages of forty-five and sixty-five. This is also the age at which one is at his peak in earnings. The majority of these people were in school from twenty to forty years ago. They still remember Christian schools 'as they were then.' They want Christian schools to be the same way now. There are many people whose perspective is rather distorted about what is spiritual. They believe that once dancing is allowed on a Christian college or university campus, it is a sign the school is deteriorating spiritually, it's backsliding, it's moving away from the Word of God. Of course, once they think a school is not proclaiming the Bible, they will not financially support it. So don't push for the right to dance, or the school will get into financial trouble." Now, it's right not to support the school if it's moving away from the Word of God. But moving toward dancing is not necessarily moving away from God's Word.

School administrators ought to level with the kids and tell them, "Personally we have nothing against dancing, we see nothing in the Scriptures which forbids you. The Word of God places emphasis on excess, and on intentions of the heart and the mind, but there is nothing morally wrong with dancing itself. But since we've got to raise money in order to keep you in school, and since we do not have the time in this particular area to argue and educate the constituency about

Keeping Spiritually Alive

their distortion from a biblical perspective, please live with our rule and regulation that there be no dancing. Please be assured we are asking you not to dance, not because we think it is unscriptural, but because it's purely a matter of economics." To me that is the more honest and just solution. I have discovered that many people oppose dancing because they never danced themselves, couldn't dance even if they wanted to, and are simply carrying over teachings that were given to them by an earlier generation for which they've never produced any profound biblical perspective.

Ultimately, whether I dance or not is not going to make all that much difference, but I do believe it is a personal thing between the individual and God. The same thing is true with playing basketball, tennis, squash, cricket, handball or Ping-Pong. It's a matter of your lifestyle being worked out between you and God. If I were attending a Christian institution which said that to attend I could not dance, and if my purpose for being at the school was far more important than the need to dance, I would make such a pledge as long as the administration understood that I wasn't abstaining in the belief that it is sinful. It is simply to live in conformity to the rules and regulations of the school in order to get out of it what I went there for.

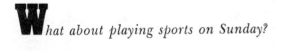

What about playing sports on Sunday?

THE BIBLE SAYS the Sabbath was made for man, not man for the Sabbath. Nothing forbids me from exercising on Sunday. Now, for many people who play sports on Sunday it's their job, their profession. For some Christians, it's their mission field.

Most of us who live in urban cities are subject to public transportation. For instance, I live in New York City and I couldn't get to fellowship with other Christians were it not for the subway, the buses, or the taxicabs. The taxicabs in New York run on Sunday, and the taxicab drivers work on Sunday. That's their job. There are subways that run on Sunday, and there are buses that run on Sunday. I've taken flights from one city to another on Sunday. If I'm going to be opposed to working on Sunday, I must also be willing to stay home on Sunday and not be subject to any form of transportation or anything that requires someone else to work to serve me, including eating in restaurants on Sunday — because the waiters and the waitresses and the cooks in the kitchen and the dishwashers and the cashiers and all those people have to work in order to serve me.

There were — and are — some outstanding Christians who went out onto the field every Sunday. Bill Glass, during his professional football career, played every Sunday afternoon with the Cleveland Browns and is now a well-known evangelist. Bobby Richardson, second baseman for the New York Yankees; Felipe Alou, a born-again believer in Jesus Christ; Charlie Harraway, fullback for the Washington Redskins, a born-again believer; Roger Staubach, quarterback for the Dallas Cowboys, a born-again believer; Fran Tarkenton, quarterback with the Minnesota Vikings, a born-again believer — every one of these fellows plays sports on Sunday.

THE PENTECOSTAL EXPERIENCE

What do you think about the Pentecostal experience in Acts 2? Is this experience valid for us today?

THE PENTECOSTAL experience is indeed valid for us today, provided we understand it. First, we must understand the ministry of the Holy Spirit. There has been a lot of discussion today about Him. There have been some tremendous movements in our country, known as "charismatic," which have penetrated far beyond the traditional, denominational Pentecostal churches into the mainline churches such as the Episcopal, the Roman Catholic, the United Methodist, and the United Presbyterian.

There are at least three major blocks of Scripture in the New Testament that deal with the ministry of the Holy Spirit. The first block is in John 14, 15, and 16 in which Jesus Christ promises the Holy Spirit. In John 14 He tells His disciples He is going away, but their hearts should not be troubled because He will not leave them comfortless; He will send to them another comforter. The word "comforter" is taken from the Greek word *parakletos,* which means one who is called alongside to aid in the time of emergency; Jesus Christ refers to Him as the Spirit of truth who "will guide you into all truth" (16:13 NIV). This means that a person who is filled with the Holy Spirit will speak the truth, live the truth, honor the truth no matter who says it. Therefore, the function of the Holy Spirit will be to bring to one's memory whatever Jesus said to him.

In John 15 Jesus says, "When the Comforter is come,...he shall testify of me" (v. 26 KJV). That is important, because of the many people connected today with the so-called charismatic movement who are making a fetish of the Holy Spirit. The emphasis should not be on the Holy Spirit; the function of the Spirit is to testify of Jesus. Therefore, any person filled with the Holy Spirit will always be speaking or pointing to Jesus Christ. John's gospel tells us more about the ministry of the Spirit when Jesus says, "The Counselor, the Holy Spirit, whom the Father will send in my name, will teach you all things and will remind you of everything I have said to you.... He will prove the world wrong about sin...because men do not believe in me; about righteousness, because I am going to the Father, where you can see me no longer; and about judgment, because the prince of this world now stands condemned" (14:26; 16:8-11 NIV).

Notice how clear the Scripture is — sin is unbelief and is the failure to stake one's life on Jesus Christ. That has nothing to do with movies or drinking or nightclubs or mini-skirts or lots of rules and regulations. The function of the Holy Spirit is to convince men of their lack of trust in Christ, which is what sin is.

Also, the Spirit will convict the world of righteousness because Jesus is going away. Jesus says He himself is righteousness personified, the perfect example of righteousness. And if He is going away, it will be necessary for Him to send the Spirit to live righteousness in us so we too can become examples of righteousness. The Holy Spirit being righteous in us will make it possible for a whole world, through the Church, to get a view of what righteousness is all about. And by the Church I mean the community of believers in Christ spread throughout the world.

Then the Holy Spirit will convince the world of judgment because the prince of this world, the devil, is judged. Contrary to many hymns, this world does not belong to Jesus Christ. Such songs as "This is my Father's world" are not theologically accurate. The Bible says the whole world is in the hands of the evil one (Rev. 12:9). Satan is "the prince of the power of the air." He is "the prince of this world." It is therefore necessary for Christians to understand that we are to be fifth columnists in Satan's world for the purpose of subverting his world with spiritual sabotage in the name of Jesus. That is why the Bible calls us out from the world. "Love not the world, neither the things that are in the world. If any man love the world, the love of the Father is not in him" (1 John 2:15 KJV). "Be not conformed to this world: but be ye transformed by the renewing of your mind" is the command of Scripture (Rom. 12:2 KJV). Satan is the prince of this world, and he and his world are under judgment. Now the Holy Spirit, through those people who are trusting Jesus Christ will convince people of sin, of righteousness, and of judgment.

The third block of Scripture is, of course, in Acts 2 and 4. Acts 2 tells actually when the Holy Spirit came on the day of Pentecost. The Bible says that when the Holy Spirit came, there were some significant conditions that existed. One: the entire church was in one accord in one place. They were not necessarily in one accord with each other; their accord was with the Lord Jesus Christ. The Word of God says, "If we walk in the light, as he is in the light, we have fellowship one with another, and the blood of Jesus Christ his Son cleanseth us from all sin" (1 John 1:7 KJV). In order to be filled with the Holy Spirit as a community of believers, this community must first be in accord with Jesus Christ, and as a result of being in one accord with Him, they will be in accord with each other. There is a geometric theorem which says that things which equal the same thing are equal to each other. That is a valid Pentecostal experience, when God's people are in accord with each other as a result of their relationship to Jesus Christ.

Another condition was that the Holy Spirit came that day as "a rushing mighty wind." Wind speaks of regeneration — the ability of God to take what is dead and make it alive. You get a glimpse of it in John 3 with Nicodemus coming to Jesus by night. Jesus confronts him by saying, "Except a man be born again, he cannot see the kingdom of God" (v. 3 KJV). Nicodemus didn't understand the new birth, and Jesus said to him, "The wind blows where it wills, and you hear the sound of it, but you do not know whence it comes or whither it goes; so it is with everyone who is born of the Spirit" (v. 8 RSV).

You see the presence of the Holy Spirit in Jesus' discussion of the new birth and by the new birth Jesus is saying a man has to be reborn in the Spirit — remade — done over. One of the functions of the Holy Spirit is to help remake a man, to regenerate him. But wind also speaks of revival, the ability of God to take what has become unconscious and renew it. You hear the prophet, for instance, as he looks across the "Valley of Dry Bones," which represents the nation of Israel which was kind of going asleep on God. The prophet cries out, "Come from the four winds, O breath, and breathe upon these slain, that they may live" (Ezek. 37:9 KJV). And so wherever God is rejuvenating His people, bringing them from unconsciousness to a state of live reality, there again is the ministry of the Holy Spirit.

The Holy Spirit also came as fire, and fire speaks of purity, the ability of God, through the Holy Spirit, to live a pure and holy life in the believer. Purity and righteousness are not our attempt to be like Jesus, but rather Jesus being Himself in us. Many people who have not experienced the fullness of the Holy Spirit are always in the continual struggle trying to live up to the Christian life, trying to produce the Christian life in their own strength and energy. Perhaps one of the greatest sins you can commit is "trying" to be a Christian. You are usurping the authority of God and the Holy Spirit. Only Jesus Christ can live His own life in us, through the power of the Holy Spirit. Righteousness, therefore, is not you trying to be like Jesus, but Jesus being Himself through you, and that is one of the ministries of the Holy Spirit in our lives.

Third, the Holy Spirit came as tongues. Now, if wind speaks of regeneration and fire speaks of purification, then tongues speak of communication. This communication goes both up and out — keeping in mind that communication is not so much what is being said as what is being heard. As these early disciples were filled with the Holy Spirit, they communicated upward, they learned how to talk to God, they learned how to

The Pentecostal Experience

praise God, they learned how to worship. A person filled with the Holy Spirit is in one continual act of praising God, making love to God, which is exactly what worship is. But it went out also. The Bible says every man in Jerusalem heard the Good News being preached in his own language. One of the tragedies of Christian religion today is that the Church does not communicate to the world in a language the world understands. We continue to communicate in a certain kind of ecclesiastical language, some kind of ecclesiastical vocabulary with only a limited number of saints understanding. The pagan society is left out. The gospel of Jesus Christ must be communicated in language and in thought patterns so the world can understand. A person filled with the Holy Spirit will communicate to his generation, in the language his generation understands, the truth about Jesus Christ.

That to me is a valid Pentecostal experience, when a person says he is filled with the Holy Spirit and is walking in the Spirit in the tradition of Pentecost. That is what we must look for. We must look for the individual's life being used to introduce other people to Jesus Christ. Other people ought to be born of the Spirit as a result of that person's life. People ought to be able to get a glimpse of the righteousness of God in that individual. That individual is constantly being relevant and constantly communicating in a language in which people can understand who Jesus Christ is and who He can be in the life of any person who dares trust Him. There are many people who, when they talk about the validity of the Pentecostal experience, demand that there be certain accompanying gifts such as "tongues." We read in 1 Corinthians 12 that there are nine gifts of the Spirit. There are "knowledge," "wisdom," "faith," "healing," "miracles," "prophecy," "discernment," "tongues," and the "interpretation of tongues." Paul exhorts us that not everyone performs miracles, not everyone heals, not everyone has wisdom, not everyone is full of knowledge. God gives gifts separately as He pleases. Simply because an individual possesses one gift, or even all nine gifts, of the Spirit is not an indication he is filled with the Spirit. The Corinthian church members would be a classic example. They had all nine gifts of the Spirit operating in the fellowship of the church, yet Paul had to address them as spiritual babies. There were people committing incest within the church — sons going to bed with their mothers. There was all kinds of carnality in the midst of that New Testament church, yet they had the gifts of the Spirit. Having the gifts of the Spirit is not an indication of being filled with the Spirit.

A manifestation of the fullness of the Spirit is written in Galatians 5:22, 23. The fruit are love, joy, peace, patience, goodness, self-control, etc. (RSV). When a person says he is filled with the Holy Spirit and says he has had a Pentecostal experience, he must show you love, he must show you joy, he must show you patience, he must show you self-control, he must show you goodness — against that, say the Scriptures, "there is no law." Possession of the gifts of the Spirit is simply an indication God is using a person. Gifts are tools God uses, but God also used the jawbone of an ass, a donkey, a raven — and if necessary, the Bible says, the rocks will cry out (Luke 19:40), and none of these objects has been known to be spiritual. God will use whom He will, and simply because an individual is being used of God does not mean he is *filled* with the Holy Spirit. We take someone in the church who is very talented, who can sing well and brings the roof down when he sings, and we say, "My, what a great man of God he is! How well he can sing!" Or we hear some eloquent preacher and we say, "What a great man of God!" What we really mean is that God is using that singer, God is using that preacher. If you want to know if he is a great man of God, you have to live with him awhile and let him show you love, joy, peace, patience. The possession of the gifts of the Spirit is not an indication that one has had a Pentecostal experience or has been filled with the Holy Spirit.

Peter gives us the clue to being filled with the Holy Spirit. In Acts 2:13, when the critics in Jerusalem saw these disciples acting and behaving rather peculiar-like on the day of Pentecost, they accused them of being drunk. But Peter said, "These

The Pentecostal Experience

men are not drunk as you suppose. It's only nine in the morning! No, this is what was spoken by the prophet Joel" (vv. 15, 16). Then in Acts 2:33 Peter says, "Therefore [that is, after having shown them that Christ was the Messiah, that Christ died and rose again from the dead and is now seated on the right hand of His Father], being by the right hand of God exalted, and having received of the Father the promise of the Holy Ghost, he hath shed forth this, which ye now see and hear" (RSV). Because Christ is exalted, the Holy Spirit is poured out. If you want to know the fullness of the Holy Spirit, it is simply a matter of letting Jesus be Lord, for every moment that Jesus Christ is Lord of your life you are filled with the Holy Spirit. Jesus gave us a further clue of what the manifestations of His lordship are. He said, "Why call ye me, Lord, Lord, and do not the things which I say?" If you are doing what Jesus is telling you, you are recognizing His lordship, and as you recognize His lordship you are filled with the Holy Spirit. That is the valid Pentecostal experience.

THE CHURCH AS THE NEW COMMUNITY

What is your attitude toward the Church, present and past?

MY PAST ATTITUDE was that the Church is an ecclesiastical system, nothing more than a social club that meets on Sunday morning, that it is a reflection of the society by which it was instituted to give theological credence to everything performed politically and economically. Now, my attitude towards the institutional church has not changed too much from that. Yet I do have a new attitude since becoming a Christian; I understand better what Jesus Christ had in mind for the Church. The word "church" is taken from the Greek word *ecclesia,* which means "called-out people." The Church is to be a live model on earth of what is happening in heaven. The Church is made of people who are committed to Jesus Christ living in fellowship with each other, in community with each other, to be vehicles through whom Jesus Christ expresses Himself. So if the world ever wants to know what is going on in heaven, all they have to do is check with us. When the world asks, "Where has love gone?" the "new community" — God's people called the Church — should be able to stand up and say, "Love is practiced here." Not theorized here, not preached here, but practiced here. When the rest of the earth's disenfranchised oppressed stand up and ask, "Where is justice?" the "new community" should be able to stand up and say, "Over here justice is practiced among us."

It was never God's intention that the Church become an institution. It was never God's intention that the Church be a rally or a social club or a political entity. The Church is to be a community of people living in relationship with each other, and that relationship is so intense it is unto death. So my attitude now is that I am both critical and excited by the

The Church as the New Community   49

Church because I'm a Churchman. I'm a product of the Church. It is through the Church that I've come to know Christ. I am an evangelist, and as an evangelist I know that evangelism begins and ends with the Church; but at the same time my commitment to the Church necessitates my criticizing it and calling it to repentance and calling it back to being a New Testament community rather than the social institution it has become in many places. I thank God there are some notable exceptions throughout the country of people who are seeking to be New Testament churches. We must get away from this idea that the Church is something that meets on Sunday morning from 11:00 to 11:59 A.M. with one minute for chimes. Rather, the Church is to be a continuous community, and by that I do not mean just the universal corporate body of Christ around the world, but I mean the local fellowships people identify with to become the visual models on earth of what's going on in heaven, and to live in community twenty-four hours a day.

Why is it that the Christian Church seems to have made much more progress in the first centuries of its history than it makes today?

THE ANSWER to that is simple. The church was illegal in the first century. You had to go underground to be in the church, because of the nature of the radical message the Christians were preaching, because it was so antisystem and so antiestablishment, and because they were being put to death for professing to be Christians — and because the values and the priorities of those people who were following Jesus Christ were in direct contradiction to the values of the system. What has happened today is that there has been a wedding between organized religion and the system. Institutions, by their very

The Church as the New Community

nature, must be entrenched in the society in which they are located and have social approval in order to exist. Since we must have social approval as churches in order to exist, it means we have to accept the priorities of the society. Thus it has grown quite popular today to be Christian, or at least religious. If we were truly doing the Jesus thing, truly confronting the world with the truth about Jesus Christ, and truly practicing justice and mercy and love, and preaching truth — living truth as Jesus Christ and His New Testament church did — we would be illegal today. You see, one of the functions of the ministry of Jesus was to destroy the works of the devil. Therefore, any person who is committed to Jesus Christ would be engaged in destroying the works of the devil, and many works of the devil are being manifested in institutional, governmental, and business forms. The oppression of Indians, Chicanos, and Blacks in America is a work of the devil. Poverty, hunger, racism, war, and militarism are works of the devil. Greed, envy, pride, and jealousy are works of the devil. Any person, therefore, who is a follower of Jesus Christ would be out to destroy these works, and he would eventually become out of step or even illegal in the kind of society in which we live. It is only under these conditions that the church could once again thrive and grow and develop and be potent — becoming the "new community," living a lifestyle, a philosophy, and having a priority that is in direct contradiction to the old system.

You have been heard to make remarks that sound very discouraging about Christianity and organized religion. Do you believe in Christianity and the institutional church?

I THINK THE answer to this question must be looked at in light of the fact there is a difference between Christianity and being Christian. I am more committed to the "Christian" part than the "ity" part. The word Christian means "Christ-In," that is, Christ in you . . . living His own life through you . . . without any help or assistance from you. The people who have Christ living in them, thus becoming what the Scriptures call a new creation in Jesus Christ, form a new community called the Church. It is these people who trust Jesus Christ and live in community with each other who form the Church.

Now, we must recognize the difference between the church with the small "c" and the Church with the capital "C." The Church with the capital "C" is that *Ecclesia,* that "called-out" people, who are committed to Jesus Christ and to each other, to be live models on earth of what is happening in heaven. The church with the small "c" is the institutional form of religion, or Christianity. Many religious institutions cannot be called the Church, but must be called simply religious institutions. That is why I prefer, when people say "I'm going down to First Presbyterian or First Episcopal Church," that they say they are going down to First Presbyterian Building or First Episcopal Building. They are not going down to the Church, because the Church is people. The Church is God's people living in community with each other.

I believe there are many institutional forms that contemporary Christianity has taken which are definitely unbiblical. Those who are seeking to be true churchmen in the New Testament sense must be at work seeking to destroy those forms that are neither relevant nor biblical. But at the same time there must be caution: some of us can become so overly critical of the institutional forms that the church has adopted that we throw the baby out with the bath water and reject the concept of the church altogether. I want to make it very clear that I am a Churchman. I am committed to the Church because it is the community of Jesus; it is the community through which Jesus Christ expresses Himself. The Church is a very valid concept because it was established by Jesus Christ Himself. Jesus gave Himself for this community called the Church, gave up His life in order to form this new community. Despite the fact I am very critical of some of the institutional forms that the Church has taken — which I believe have become cumbersome, too mechanical, too denominational and sectarian — I honestly believe and am committed to the Church as a concept, in the building of a new community.

Will society ever see the year 2000 in view of the enormous problems facing it?

IT WOULD BE difficult for me to say that society will end at all based on how big the problems are. It will not be the problems that determine the end of society, but rather the decadence of man. There is no indication in Scripture that the whole society — that is, all the people in the world — is doomed to annihilation. The Bible does talk about the end of Gentile rule — that is, the end of the rule of those people who are alienated from God. Now, as to the exact date when this will happen, it is the time of the second coming of Jesus, the time of the establishment of His kingdom on earth, when He shall rule for ever and ever. I cannot see such a date. I can say that, based on the signs of the times — that is, based on what is happening sociologically and economically in the world today and based on what Scripture says will happen in the "last days" — we are definitely moving toward some sort of cataclysmic rendezvous with destiny.

My function as a Christian is to be more occupied with bringing about the kingdom of God on earth, through being a live model as well as by communicating the claims of Jesus Christ to as many people as possible who will listen. I must carry out the ministry of Jesus Christ and leave the rest to God. So that I don't become entangled with dates of the second coming of Jesus Christ, neither do I get myself hung up on too many eschatological questions.

What *do you believe about the second coming of the Lord Jesus Christ?*

PERHAPS ONE of the most important teachings of the New Testament is the concept of the return of Jesus Christ. In the New Testament alone it is mentioned more than 218 times. When Jesus Christ arose from the dead, He spent approximately 40 days with His disciples and then, the Bible says, He ascended back to heaven. The disciples stood gazing as Jesus Christ went up, and an angel stood by and said, "Why stand ye gazing? This same Jesus will come back the same way He has gone." The disciples preached this. In fact, the disciples were so intense about it that they honestly believed Jesus Christ would return in their generation. They preached what has become known as "the imminent return of Jesus Christ." Of course, we know some of them were wrong because it has been 1,900 years. Nevertheless, the teaching is valid. Jesus Christ Himself told His disciples to occupy until He comes. This means that, while the return of Jesus Christ is valid and real, the church is to spend less time being occupied with His coming; less time being obsessed with His coming; and more time being occupied with His work...until He returns. Because what will usher in the return of Jesus Christ is the establishment of His kingdom on earth — in the hearts of men who trust Him.

It is in this vein that a great number of people in recent days have become quite concerned about what theologians call "eschatological questions." One of the top-selling religious books today is one written by Hal Lindsey, entitled *The Late Great Planet Earth,* in which he talks about prophetic and

54   *The Church as the New Community*

future things in the Scriptures. I am not one to become involved in any kind of debate or discussion on when Jesus Christ is coming back, because the Bible is quite plain when it states no one knows the hour in which the Son of Man will return. There is much discussion in certain Christian circles about these being the last days, that all the signs we have around us are evidence Jesus Christ is coming soon. I don't know about that; I can't tell you whether it's going to be another 1,000 years or 2,000 years or whether Jesus Christ is coming back next week, or next year. I will not bring discredit to the name of Jesus, as some people have, in trying to predict dates. I will tell you that Scripture is quite definite in its teaching that Jesus Christ will return to the earth to establish on earth His kingdom. "He shall reign for ever and ever" and "the kingdom of this world has become the kingdom of our Lord and of his Christ" (NIV).

YOUTH IN SOCIETY

Why can't the youth of today find the answers to their problems with God?

THE FACT IS, my friend, that many young people *are* finding Christ as the answer to their problems. There is a tremendous movement of the Holy Spirit going on among young people in America today. And it just may well be that the young people in America are going to change this country. An outstanding evangelical seminary located in Massachusetts has a student body of which more than 60 percent have become Christians only within the last five or six years. This is also true of a number of other seminaries which are preparing people to communicate faith in Jesus Christ in our time. In fact, more young people than adults are turning to God today.

Not only is there much discussion among young people and a kind of revival of religion among them, but also religion is becoming a fad in many circles. The whole Jesus Revolution occurring today involves a great number of young people. Now, I must confess there is a difference between what is authentic among them and what is a fad, because Jesus is vogue for many. Not long ago the two top Broadway plays were both related to Jesus Christ; one was *Godspell* and the other was *Jesus Christ Superstar*. There has been a lot of Jesus music around: Don Hathaway singing "He Ain't Heavy, He's My Brother"; Roberta Flack singing "Sunday and Sister Jones"; again Roberta Flack singing "I Told Jesus He Could Change My Name"; Judy Collins's rendition of "Amazing Grace" several years ago. There has been a tremendous Jesus revival among youth, and many of them are getting into Christ and discovering He is more than just a fad, more than just a superstar, but truly Lord.

Youth in Society 59

Do *you think it is because the younger generation is better educated today that we are having all this rebellion and strife? How come we did not have this in other generations? Are there some other reasons?*

FIRST OF ALL, we have had rebellion in other generations. It's just that each generation has had its own form of rebellion. You must keep in mind that the man who rode through the villages crying "The British are coming! The British are coming!" was part of a rebellion against British authority. The people who threw bricks and bottles at police on King Street in Boston in the mid-1770s were also young people who were rebelling. The army that George Washington led was an army of young people rebelling against British authority. Two generations ago our fathers invaded girls' dormitories in panty raids. They also had these ridiculous things in seeing how many people could be stuffed into a telephone booth — they wrecked more telephone booths that way — because that was their form of rebellion. Young people today rebel by taking drugs. Our parents rebelled by drinking — and became alcoholics. I have asked myself, What's the difference?

I do believe, though, that young people today are more enlightened, and education does have something to do with it because young people are more informed than their parents. They're more informed about the injustices and inequities in our society. The problem, of course, is that they have all this knowledge about how messed-up the system is, but they do not have the strength, the ability, or the know-how to change it. They feel frustrated.

Another reason for rebellion among young people today that did not occur in other generations is that they are not as afraid as their parents were. In past generations, the system had such economic control over people that they would be afraid to rebel against any of its injustices or inequities because of the reprisals that could be brought against them. Today a lot more young people have experienced affluence as children; they have been brought up in an affluent society. In fact, they have become bored with affluence, and because of their boredom with it they are not frightened by the threat of losing social position or status. Many of them are really not that interested in succeeding in the system on the system's terms. Some of them are more interested in freedom and the ability to express themselves than in the kind of moral prostitution that must occur in order for them to rise on the social and economic ladder in the system. Thus, because — unlike their parents — they are no longer threatened or intimidated by the system, they feel free to rebel against it.

Generations Apart," a TV documentary, pointed out through surveys that college young people are more revolutionary and more militant and less patriotic than most of the young people the same age who do not attend college. Therefore, do you feel college can be a hindrance rather than a help both emotionally and spiritually to the average individual?

BECAUSE A PERSON is revolutionary, because a person is militant, and because a person is not patriotic does not mean he is not spiritual. I am committed to Jesus Christ. I love Him with all my heart. I believe that the Scriptures are the Word of God and that the only means to a redeemed society is our society coming to grips with who Jesus Christ is and who He can be in us, both individually and collectively. I am a revolutionary. To be a revolutionary is to take an existing situation which has proven to be unworkable, archaic, and impractical and to put it down and replace it with a system that works.

The Word of God says, "Therefore if any man be in Christ, he is a new creature; old things are passed away; behold all things are become new" (2 Cor. 5:17 KJV). That makes the gospel of Jesus Christ revolutionary. To be militant is to be aggressive. To be militant is to be angry about injustice, to be angry about sin, to be angry about those things which God does not intend to be inflicted upon men, and to oppose them with all one's might. To that extent I am militant. Militancy is disciplined by the Holy Spirit and the Word of God. I would be considered by many right-wing people in this country to be unpatriotic. I do not believe America was founded by God. I do not believe God is the chairman of the Republican or the Democrat Party or the head of the Joint Chiefs of Staff or super-capitalist extraordinary, nor is He the head of any other system. I will not wear a bumper sticker on my car saying, SUPPORT GOD AND COUNTRY. I do not believe in God-country-mamma-the-girl-back-home-and-apple-pie. Now, that does not make me an anarchist. That does not make me a Communist, nor does it make me unpatriotic. It simply means I'm facing up to reality.

This country was founded by pagans, like any other nation. There were Christians on the *Mayflower* who came over and settled in this country, but the people who wrote our Constitution and established this government—Thomas Jefferson, Thomas Paine, Alexander Hamilton, George Washington— these fellows were not Christians. They were Deists. None of them believed in personal salvation through Jesus Christ. None of them believed that through the death and resurrection of Jesus Christ man can be redeemed. When Patrick Henry stood up and said, "Give me liberty or give me death!" he might have had his mind blown if two or three dozen of his slaves had said, "Me too!" If God runs this country, that makes God the enemy. That means God is responsible for the massacre of hundreds of thousands of Indians; that God has been responsible for breaking all the treaties with them, driving them from their land, almost extinguishing them; that God has been responsible for the lynching of more than 10,000 black people in this country in the last eighty years, that we know about; that God is responsible for the oppression of other groups in this country. It makes God responsible for 1 percent of the population in America having 39 percent of all the stock, 43 percent of all the cash; and 1 percent of the businesses in America making 70 percent of all the profits. To say that God is responsible for that lopsided situation and that God dropped bombs on people makes God the enemy. God doesn't run this country — and never has. That is why it is very difficult to salute the American flag with integrity with a pledge that says, "One nation under God." We are not one nation, and we're not under God. God doesn't run the United States Congress, God doesn't run the United States Senate, God doesn't run the White House. I don't care how many prayer meetings they have in the Oval Room. God doesn't run our state legislatures, God doesn't even run a whole lot of our churches. Putting God's name on our money, "In God We Trust," may be an ideal for some, maybe hopefully that's what we're like, but that is not the case. It is not in God we trust, it's the coin on which God's name is that we trust. We trust in General Motors, we trust in General Electric, we trust in IBM, we trust in Eastman Kodak, we trust in missiles and planes and bombs — we do not trust in God.

If young people are finding this out in college (I didn't know they were discovering these truths in *college*), then praise God. Learning the truth about this country has nothing to do with spirituality. It will help young people to find out there is no hope but in Jesus Christ. In fact, I'm glad when young people discover the truth about America, the truth about what we really trust, and really learn how this country is run. When they discover this is really a pagan nation, it provides the opportunity to confront people with the lordship of Jesus Christ, to change their allegiances from these messed-up props, and to put their confidence in the Lord.

For the last few years I've noticed the sexual immorality of young people has increased immensely. How are the young people to conquer this problem? What must we do to prevent further degeneration?

I PERSONALLY don't believe sexual immorality is any greater among young people today than in any other generation. It is just that there are more young people, and so there is more immorality it seems. What you are seeing today is greater freedom and discussion of sex — some liberated attitudes about sex and a more open display of what I consider degradation of what God intended sex to be. For instance, magazines and books are sold on the newsstands that could not have been sold openly years ago. They were still being sold, but not on the open market as they are today. So I think we have to distinguish between a more liberated attitude about sex, or free discussion about sex, and sexual immorality. I believe the problem of immorality was great forty years ago, and it is great today. It hasn't just changed; it's simply that people are more bold about it, a little more open about it. Years ago people committed as much adultery as is committed today; but more people are being open and discussing it, whereas they hid it several years ago. It is also necessary to understand that the real hangup with sexual immorality is not simply that two bodies come together. God probably doesn't get uptight because two human bodies unite; but He is concerned when relationships are violated. A relationship becomes immoral when proper relationships are violated by that act.

One of the best ways to prevent sexual decay in American society is to educate our children properly at home and in the church. It is a tragedy that Christian churches have not generally fostered an attitude toward sex other than "Don't, don't, don't"! and haven't brought people together to talk about the beauty of sex and the exciting relationship that occurs in sexual intercourse within the confines of God's law. Churches were not in generations past, and are not now, equipped to educate our young people from a biblical perspective about the excitement of sex, the beauty of sex, the truth of sex, biologically, emotionally, and mentally — because of their vast ignorance on the subject. Yet there have been some attempts at this. One book I recommend to you to give your children is Charlie Shedd's, entitled *The Stork Is Dead*.

Do *you think parents should allow kids to wear clothes and hair in a way that would please their friends? Why? Why not?*

THE WORD OF GOD exhorts us, "Whatever you do, do it for the glory of God" (1 Cor. 10:31 NIV). The wearing of clothes, aside (at times) from being a moral issue, is also a cultural and social issue. Many of us wear our clothes based on the dictate of our particular culture. None of us in the 1970s dress the way our parents did in the '30s or our grandparents did at the turn of the century. I think many of us as adults have to confess that we dress according to our particular cultural idiosyncrasies. We must be open to the fact that young people today dress differently according to their peer groups. Many times as parents we want our kids to dress to satisfy our own social group and cannot tolerate them dressing to satisfy theirs. Many young people today want to wear dungarees, old shirts, and sandals — and I see no reason why they shouldn't. The Word of God talks about dressing in modesty, and that has to do with not being too ostentatious. You can draw attention to yourself by being too pietistic as well as being too super-mod. Persons must find the medium range in which they dress without bringing too much attention to themselves, yet without being too pietistic or being so super-chic that they don't reflect the nature of their Spirit or the spirit of Christ.

SOCIAL RESPONSIBILITY

Don't you think that if people are engaged in preaching the Word of God they will not have time to get involved in all these social issues?

I DO NOT SEE how a person could read the Word of God and be willing to obey it and not become socially responsible. The Scriptures call us not only to be hearers of the Word but to be doers also. Jesus Himself said, "Why do you call me, 'Lord, Lord,' and do not do what I say?" (Luke 6:46 NIV).

This whole issue about the Social Gospel had its roots well over a hundred years ago when a man by the name of Walter Rauschenbusch wrote a position paper entitled "The Social Gospel," in which he argued for those people who would be the followers of Jesus Christ to also become actively engaged in meeting the social needs of people. Immediately this produced a dichotomy within the church — a struggle between what are known as the liberals and the conservatives. The liberals (a label I don't like) and the conservatives (another label I don't like) went at each other, the liberals arguing that God has called us to become engaged in being socially redemptive, that we must feed hungry people, that we must put clothes on naked people's backs, we must deal with slums, we must deal with seeking to redeem man from an oppressed society. On the other hand, the conservatives said, "You know our job is to preach the Word, preach the Gospel. Our job is to give people a passport out of hell to heaven. Our job is to call men to repentance and salvation in Jesus Christ, but we will not get involved in any of these social issues." The liberal said, "No, we've got to feed hungry people," and the conservative said, "No, we've got to preach the Gospel," until at last both of them have gone to extremes and neither is correct.

Any classic study of man will let us know that man, while being one person, has many aspects to him — mental, emotional, spiritual, physical. If we're talking about saving this man, we must talk about saving his entire being. We must talk about redeeming his entire being. The Apostle Paul understood this when he said we should not be conformed to this world but be transformed by the renewing of one's mind (Rom. 12:1, 2), because Paul understood that as a man thinks in his heart, so is he. That part of salvation is mentally redeeming man from the processes, priorities, and irrational thinking of the world's system to a more rational standard, which is the kingdom of God. Jesus was committed to this kind of salvation when He said people ought to be made whole, because Jesus held to a holistic view of man rather than to compartmentalizing him to certain aspects and demanding only that one aspect of him be redeemed. On one hand, the Bible talks about spiritual hell for those who fail to believe on Jesus Christ. The function of those who are preachers and communicators of the Bible, and the function of the entire church community, is to call men out of spiritual darkness, out of spiritual hell, to the lordship and the authority of Jesus Christ. (Man is a very spiritual person, and much of his motivation, his drive, and his thinking process is spiritual.) On the other hand, it is very difficult to call people to a renewing of their minds if they do not have the capacity to renew their minds, or even to grasp or understand, because they are physically limited. For instance, we know the lack of protein in a person's diet inhibits growth, prohibits the brain from functioning at its fullest capacity. It inhibits a lot of intellectual as well as physical development. So if we deny a man protein, which doesn't allow his brain to develop, how is he going to rationally figure out the truth when the Holy Spirit communicates it to him? Obviously God intends for man to have protein as well as the truth. James is very clear on this point when he talks about a man knocking at one's door and this man is naked and cold and hungry. You can't just open the door, stand there, and say, "In the name of Jesus be warm, in the name of Jesus be clothed, in the name of Jesus be fed." You have to invite the man into the house and feed him. He can't be warm simply because you declare it to be so.

In the same way, it is impossible to be committed to Jesus Christ and not have social responsibility. Any parent who is a Christian has social responsibility to raise his kids, feed them, see that they are educated, protect them, and bring them up in the fear and admonition of the Lord. This escapism on the part of some people who merely say, "Just preach the Word," is no good if the Word doesn't take form, if it doesn't have flesh, if it doesn't express itself, if it doesn't work itself out in relationships between man and man (and between man and God), if it does not forge the new community. Therefore, the person who only wants to give me a passport out of hell to heaven is preaching an extreme Gospel because he wants only to save something called my spirit (my soul) and I am more than spirit. On the other hand, my liberal friend wants only to feed my belly. And I'm also more than a belly. Both persons dehumanize me.

I suppose a way to illustrate this is to have you take a piece of paper and a pencil and draw a circle. At the top of the circle put the word "God." At the bottom of the circle put the word "community." On the left side put the term "personal salvation." On the right side, "social salvation." Now, to illustrate the extremes, one group starts from God and moves left to personal salvation. They call people to repentance, they tell them they must accept Jesus Christ as their Savior, and they seek to explain to them the claims of Jesus Christ spiritually upon their lives — but they stop there. These people are the "personal salvationists." The other group moves from God and goes right to social salvation. They become actively engaged in feeding hungry people, clothing naked people. They take part in establishing social agencies to try to redeem a messed-up society. They become involved with all the social implications of the kingdom — but they stop at that point. Neither group gets around to the other side. Neither one forms community; the social salvationist and the personal salvationist both fail to form a community to execute the whole plan of God. The social salvationist never gets around to calling men to personal redemption, and the personal salvationists never get around to calling people to corporate or community salvation. And so they all end up preaching only one aspect of the Gospel.

The person who would represent Jesus Christ with a more holistic view must be calling people to personal repentance as well as to corporate fellowship and social salvation. One of my functions as a preacher of the Gospel is to be a catalyst to seek to bring about a marriage between the social activist and the salvationist — to allow the salvationist to know that if he is only calling people out of hell to heaven, he is preaching only part of the Gospel; and to tell the social activist that if he is only feeding hungry people and clothing naked people, he is preaching only one aspect of the Gospel. They must be doing the whole thing to have a whole ball of wax. This is exactly what was personified in Jesus Christ.

You place a great emphasis on social responsibility on the part of the person who would follow Jesus Christ. Isn't it possible to become so sensitive to people's needs that we become less sensitive to what God wants in our lives?

I AM AMAZED you would make a dichotomy. It seems to me it would be impossible to be insensitive to God and yet be sensitive to the real needs of other people. To be sensitive to other people's needs, to me, is to be sensitive to God. James implies, "How can we say that we love God when we cannot love the people whom we deal with every day?" This is one of the shameful aspects of the whole institutional Christianity: to be so absorbed with God and so insensitive to other people.

How could a man put on a hood, go out and join the Ku

Klux Klan and lynch black people, and at the same time be holding up the King James Version and saying he believes the Bible is the Word of God and "be willing to break his right arm in order to prove it"? Or, how in South Africa could Christians claim to be committed to God and not be committed to the people whom God is committed to? It is unfortunate that we have produced a religious theology devoid of a practical outlook. It is impossible to be in right relationship to God and not be in right relationship with man.

One of the problems with a great number of people's insensitivity to other people is that they have never been able to strip the truth about Jesus Christ from its cultural trappings. We tend to deal with Jesus Christ within the confines of our particular cultural idiosyncrasies. If we are Norwegian, we try to make God Norwegian. If we are African, we try to make God African. If we are American, we try to make God American. If we are British, we try to make God British. We always try to view God within the cultural framework we grew up in. But we can't do this because God must be dealt with on the basis of truth, devoid of cultural trappings. If He is to be interpreted and proclaimed, He must be interpreted and proclaimed within the cultural context we are communicating through. But truth should always be rid of cultural snags.

You see, cultures are not superior or inferior to each other; they are simply different. There are different fashions, different thought processes, different music and art. But the art and music of one culture is not inferior or superior to another; it is simply different. The rationale, then, is that I seek to compute or inject into God or have God inject into other people my particular cultural tastes and preferences. For instance, if I like Bach, Beethoven, and Chopin as musical styles, I might assume that since I'm a Christian and I like Bach and Beethoven, God wants everyone to appreciate Bach and Beethoven. If the kind of clothes I wear are dark clothes generally on the conservative side, I would therefore assume, since I'm a Christian, that all people who are Christian should wear dark, conservative clothing.

Some people who claim to be followers of Jesus Christ have a way of seeking to impose all the cultural idiosyncrasies they have, since they are Christians, on other people. So they assume that other people who do not adopt their cultural idiosyncrasies are not Christians. This, of course, is contrary to Scripture. I am an American. I consider myself a Christian. I consider myself a Spirit-filled Christian. Therefore, it would seem to me that all true Christians ought to be American. I'm a capitalist, and I consider myself a Spirit-filled Christian. Therefore, all Spirit-filled Christians ought to be capitalists... and on and on go the arguments. That is why we have a great number of people who have taken God and wrapped Him up in the American flag, made Him president of the New York Stock Exchange, chairman of the Republican party, and head of the Joint Chiefs of Staff. That's why we believe God is on our side, and that's why we have people with bumper stickers on their cars saying, "Support God and Country," as if they go together. They honestly believe that what they are committed to, God is committed to.

We also did this with slavery in America. You see, slavery was politically and economically feasible. You could buy a healthy male slave for $600 and a healthy female slave for $300. They were made to cohabit. The woman became pregnant and bore chidren. After a while you ended up with quite a number of slaves. It made possible cheap labor for the cotton fields, for cotton was the king industry at that particular time. In American society, what is economically feasible is politically feasible, and to uphold that immorality politically and economically we needed the church to give its theological sanction to slavery. So many people preached that slavery was a divine institution of God and that God had cursed black people and relegated them to conditions of servitude. Thus those people who were Christians and wanted to benefit from the slave system found a loophole. They honestly believed they had theological credence and divine unction and authority to maintain the slave system, because people will always find a way to try to prove that God supports the particular cultural objective they have in mind, even though it might be in total contradiction to what God is all about.

Since we want to make the world safe for democracy (and we believe that to do this we have to drop bombs on innocent Southeast Asians), we have to say that God is for this, so we even have prayer meetings in the Pentagon. We pray God will give our pilots who drop these B52 bombs on the Vietnamese people divine safety to return home. "Lord, bomb out the enemy; don't leave any of them." We honestly believe we can inject God into almost any objective we set ourselves to here in America. The tragedy is, the people who claim to belong to the new community called the Church, who are supposed to be the prophets to the system, end up supporting the system.

Isn't it true that from this new community you are talking about there will emerge a new culture?

THE ANSWER naturally is Yes. Out of the commitment one has to Jesus Christ will emerge new priorities, new values, and new expressions within that community. The difference between this and the way the system operates is that the culture in the system cannot be changed unless you reorder the priorities in it. Because of our commitment to Jesus Christ and His becoming our Lord, we've formed this new community called the Church. It means our poetry, our music, our fashions, the way we do things, will have their frame of reference within Jesus Christ, thus having a profound impact on our cultural expression. Our cultural expressions ought to grow up out of our relationship with Jesus Christ, rather than first having a cultural expression and then trying to relate it to Jesus. Again, I want to make it clear that God speaks through culture, and chooses to use the various cultural forms that exist in order to have Himself expressed. We must not say that because God is being expressed through a culture, it makes the culture Christian.

CHANGING THE SYSTEM

ow can we young people become actively engaged in changing the system?

THERE ARE MANY adults and parents who are always concerned when we use the word "system," because they think the people who talk about changing the system are generally Communists, anarchists, or rebellious people. Those of us of biblical persuasion, when we talk about the "system," think of the world order, the order of things, the way they exist in what is called the cosmos of the world's system.

The Bible says the whole world's system lies in the hands of the evil one. The Bible is quite clear about the fact that Satan is the "prince of this world." Now, of course, when we start talking about Satan or the devil, people get upset and disturbed because they have pictures of some cat in a red jumpsuit with a funny leer on his face and a pitchfork in his hand, a tail, and horns growing out of his forehead. That is not what we mean when we talk about the devil. We are talking about a spirit of superhuman resourcefulness, who has set himself up in diametric opposition to the plan and purpose of God. In fact, the Bible says he is the god of this world, and God has not removed him from that position. He is the ultimate oppressor.

We have to accept the fact that God has pronounced judgment on all the systems of men. This is why it is important for people to understand that God is not a capitalist, a socialist, nor a Communist. God is not a left-winger or a right-winger; God is not a Democrat or a Republican; God is neither for the East nor for the West; but rather, He is the Lord of heaven and earth who has come to establish His own thing. What He has come to do is to destroy the works of the devil and to build His kingdom on earth in the hearts of men.

When we talk about changing the system, then we have only three alternatives:

(1) We can talk about getting together and bombing out the system. That isn't feasible, because bombing out the system really means only bombing the facilities of the system, destroying the facilities of the system merely inconveniences the system — but it doesn't change it. A guy puts a bomb under a General Motors plant, and then says, "We got General Motors, we blew up General Motors." He hasn't touched General Motors, because tomorrow morning the Executive Committee of General Motors will meet to find a new location to build a new plant. They will double production facilities in several other plants to make up for the loss of production in the one that was bombed. The insurance will cover the building of a new plant, and what that doesn't cover will be written off on next year's income tax. So, you haven't really touched General Motors.

(2) Then there are those people who say they will go into the system and try to change it from within. To me this is a fallacious argument because there is no such breed of cats. Nobody has ever changed the system from within. The nature of this oppressive world's system that we live in is such that to change it from within you must first get into it. Then you have to work yourself up to a position of power, so that you can have authority to effect a change. But in working yourself up into the position of power where you can effect change, you have had to so prostitute yourself in the process that you forgot what you came there for. I remember that several years ago, while at college, I used to talk to a lot of the guys who were planning on going into the ministry. They were all talking about how they were going to change the church's systems when they went in, and how, when they became pastors, they were going to radicalize the church and make it more relevant and contemporary. When I travel across the country and ask them how they are doing in changing their churches now that they are pastors, they don't even remember

Changing the System

holding the conversation about changing the system, far less doing it. Now that they have become part of the church system or the religious system they've discovered it has changed them. You see, it is very difficult to change any system — be it political, ecclesiastical, or economical — from the inside. It is also very difficult to change any system that is writing your paycheck.

(3) Some of us can get together and build live models of what the system ought to be. To me that is the only viable solution; in essence, that is what the church is supposed to be about — getting together and becoming live alternatives to the present system. That is the only way to effect change.

In the light of this, what then should be our relationship, that is, the relationship to the old system of those of us who are building these live models of new communities?

OUR RELATIONSHIP is that we infiltrate it. Jesus told His disciples that they were to be *in* the system but not *of* the system. Jesus Christ said, "Love not the system, neither the things that are in the system because if you love the system then the love of the Father is not in you" (cf. 1 John 2:15). The Apostle Paul tells us in Romans 12:1, "Don't allow the system to press you into its mold, but be transformed by the renewing of your minds" (cf. Phillips). But at the same time Jesus Christ said, "Go ye therefore into all the system and preach the Gospel" (cf. Mark 16:15). Therefore, we have to be in this system, but not of it. Many of us will be called to serve in various aspects of the system, not in the terms of helping to affirm it, but in becoming infiltrators, fifth columnists in the system for the purpose of subverting the system in the name of Jesus. We subvert the system with love, we subvert the system with justice, we subvert the system with the light of Jesus Christ, we subvert it with His life, we subvert it by being the vehicles through which He expresses Himself.

Some of us will be called to be professional athletes, and we will represent the new community in the athletic world. Some of us will be called to be businessmen, not just to make money, not just for the stock options and the other benefits that the company offers, but for the purpose of infiltrating the business world in the name of Jesus to confront people with the new community and Jesus Christ. Some of us will be educators, others will be sociologists, psychologists, and what-have-you. The purpose of the new community called the Church is to equip the people in the fellowship of the Church for that kind of ministry.

Perhaps one of the most tragic terms used in Christian circles today is the term "full-time Christian service." There should be no such thing. Every person, according to the Scriptures, should be a minister of the Gospel, full-time, engaged in confronting people with Jesus Christ and being a live model on earth of what is happening in heaven. Therefore, the company you work in, the athletic team you play for, the school you teach in, or the street you collect garbage on is your mission field. This is the place God has put you to be the representative of Jesus Christ, to infiltrate the world's system in the name of Jesus.

Jesus Christ said to those who represent Him, to the new community, that they are to be the salt of the earth. Salt has three significant characteristics:

(1) Salt creates thirst. Infiltrating a sick world's system, we — by our lifestyle — will create in people who are bound by this system a thirst for the freedom that they see we have in Christ, and they will become thirsty for the living God.

(2) Salt penetrates without losing its saltiness. The purpose of the Christian is that he must penetrate the world's system without becoming like the world's system.

(3) Salt preserves. Those who are the salt of the earth will preserve justice, mercy, love, and the acts of the Holy Spirit on the earth.

Changing the System

ow can we keep the system from becoming more dehumanizing and oppressive than it already is?

THERE ARE A couple of things that can be done, but it is going to require a change in the priorities on the part of those people who want to prevent the system from becoming more dehumanizing. One step, of course, is to hit the system where it hurts, that is, in the pocketbook. Black people have discovered, for instance, that this can be done with various supermarkets and food stores who charge more for food in the black communities than in the white communities. By boycotting these stores and refusing to buy from them on a mass scale, you force the store economically to become more just and more human. I believe black people could do this with General Motors. Black people buy enough Cadillacs and Buicks to have a definitely devastating effect on the profits of General Motors in those two divisions. Therefore, if General Motors is refusing to make movements conducive to the development of the black community, black people should consider that.

Young people today who are talking about trying to humanize the system in the area of war could have brought the war to an end a long time ago if they had brought economic pressure on the system. For instance, young people between the ages of sixteen and twenty-four were the group of people most opposed to the war; and those young people in 1972 spent something like $18 billion on phonograph records. All young people in America had to do was to serve notice on the record industry that until the war was over they were not going to buy any more phonograph records — and the record industry would have ended the war for them. They wouldn't have had to march, demonstrate, or anything.

Another method is that every time the system does something immoral, there must be those who become prophets to the system, who stand up and cry out with a loud voice through every means possible to warn people about what the system is doing. This must be done through newspapers, this must be done on television, this must be done by radio, this must be done by word of mouth, it must be done in the classroom. There must be enough people committed to constantly putting up red flags every time the system dehumanizes somebody. This can prevent the system from becoming more dehumanizing than it already is. It is only then, when a significant number of us can change our priorities and values, that we can effectively begin "humanizing" the system.

We are seeing some of this happen today. For instance, a lot of young women are giving the mink and fur business fits, simply because young women are not interested in owning stoles any longer, whereas in the last generation the crowning achievement of a man's commitment to his wife was to buy her a mink coat. That's all changed in this generation. We've changed the clothing industry. Young people are not getting dressed in the usual business form that we knew in a previous generation, so they have forced the fashion industry's concept of clothing and manufacturing to change. We are capable of effectively changing the system if we are willing to change our priorities and values.

I'm afraid though, that many young people want to see the system changed, but are not willing to make sacrifices necessary to bring about those changes. We aren't prepared to give up our phonograph records. We are not prepared to make the financial sacrifices. We are not prepared to give up possible status and recognition in the system. We become so victimized by the system and have such a deep-seated need to be accepted that most of us will end up going into the system and accepting its priorities and values, thus negating any opportunity for true revolution in American society.

Doesn't the system force us to conform to its standards in order to infiltrate it for Jesus' sake? For instance, in dress one must dress a particular way to go to school, one must dress a particular way to go in business. Suppose that as a Christian I have my own individual taste, but the system will not allow me to participate in it if I do not wear its uniform. Even Christians today are getting very strict on this question of dress. What should we do in this instance?

WELL, IT IS TRUE that the system, as well as many Christians who have adopted the cultural standards of the system, has some distorted ideas about codes of dress. For example, for a long time the only way you could succeed on Wall Street or in any kind of conservative business was that you had to wear a dark suit, what was considered to be a business tie, and a white shirt. In fact, white shirts were the only shirts that could be worn. Over the recent years we have been able to start wearing colored shirts — blue, red, brown, and many other colors. But even there it is beginning to drift back to white. One executive at IBM sometime ago forced all of his executives to return to white shirts, ties, and very conservative apparel because he believed it to be commensurate with the dignity of business attire.

Many so-called Christians have been debating for centuries the whole question of code of dress, particularly as it applies to women — where the sleeves ought to fall, where the hemline ought to fall, where the neckline ought to fall. This, of course, produces some real problems because the Bible gives us the standard by which dress should be dealt with. It talks about how women ought to dress with modesty. Now the question is, "What is modest?" This is dictated, first, by the attitude and intentions of the dresser, and second, by the cultural idiosyncrasies of the society at that particular point in human history. For instance, during my father's generation, men would get very excited and sexually stimulated by the sight of a woman's ankle. When a woman stepped out of a carriage or a car and some of her ankles showed, men would wolf-whistle and make all kinds of sensual noises. Of course, in our generation we have to see a little bit more than a woman's ankle to be turned on. The people in each generation become accustomed to what they see and become less stimulated by it.

In one school in New York City several years ago, before the maxiskirts became popular, a young girl showed up at school wearing a maxidress. She was wolf-whistled and followed all over the school by scores of young men. Halfway through the day she created such a disturbance wearing this full length maxidress (because the guys were stimulated by what they could not see), the principal called her down to his office, forced her to go home, made her change. She put on a miniskirt, came back to school, and everything was okay. The fellows in the school had become accustomed to seeing miniskirts and were no longer stimulated by seeing girls' legs and their bare thighs. The fact that this girl wore a maxiskirt and stimulated the fellows by what they could not see shows you that one must always decide what the nature of the society is in order to determine what is modest or immodest.

I think a great number of missionaries made this mistake overseas. We were sent overseas to communicate the claims of Jesus Christ, but once Africans came to know Christ we also told them those little two-piece things they wore around their waists were no longer appropriate — they had to wear pants like the rest of us in the Western world. But God didn't send us to Africa to convert people to Western clothes, He sent us to Africa to convert people to Jesus Christ. There is a difference. In Southeast Asia, for instance, Polynesian women or other women go around with their breasts exposed. It's not uncommon for a mother to feed her child in the road or in public vehicles of transportation. It's a common sight to see a

Changing the System

woman with her breasts exposed in the South Pacific and in Southeast Asia. When the missionaries began to preach Jesus Christ, many of these women came to know Him and were told, "Now that you have accepted Jesus Christ you too must wear a Playtex." But Jesus Christ didn't send us to the South Pacific to tell women about bras; He sent us to tell them about Himself. It did not occur to the missionary that a woman's breast in those countries is not a sex symbol as it is in the Western world. It also didn't occur to the missionary that Southeast Asian men were not climbing a wall because they could see the women's breasts. The missionary was climbing the wall and wouldn't admit it.

Therefore, it is very necessary, when we interpret Scripture with reference to "Women should adorn themselves with modesty," that we do so with understanding of modesty within the cultural limitations of the present age and generation, and within the intentions and attitude of the dresser, as well as within the dictates of his conscience as saturated with the Holy Spirit and the Word of God. I do not believe we can set a uniform standard of dress for everyone. The shape of one's body — how big one is, how skinny, or how fat — must help determine one's dress. The cultural idiosyncrasies of the particular society in which the individual is operating must also be considered. There must not be, there cannot be, a uniform standard of dress for all people.

When it comes to infiltrating or participating in the system, we must recognize that there are certain things we might have to do for Jesus' sake that are not necessarily moral compromise. This is what Paul meant when he said, "I have become all things to all men so that by all possible means I might save some" (1 Cor. 9:22 NIV). There is the illustration of Paul's sending Timothy up to Jerusalem to preach. Paul said, "Timothy, you must get yourself circumcised." Timothy very easily put up the argument, "But, Paul, you've already told us there is neither circumcision nor uncircumcision; it doesn't make a difference because circumcision has nothing to do with salvation." Paul said, "Yes, I know, but the people to whom you are going to be preaching in Jerusalem are hung up on circumcision. So that they will be able to hear your communication about Christ, get circumcised."

If I'm invited to communicate the Gospel of Jesus Christ to a very conservative group of midwestern businessmen, I know something about those men. I know they are extremely patriotic, very conservative, they are formed out of a particular mold. And while I might like to go dressed in casual dress because I feel much more comfortable casually dressed, I know they would be much more occupied with what I have on than with the message I was delivering. It is much more important that my message get across than that I be allowed to have my own way about my clothing. So I would put on a business suit, a white shirt, and a business tie, and fit right into the mold so that the radical message I have to preach will go across unhindered. I believe those of us who want to infiltrate the system with Jesus must be open to some of these tactics.

THE ROLE OF THE BLACK CHURCH

What is the role of the black church in the black man's struggle for liberation?

THE BLACK CHURCH has historically been the most powerful social institution in the black community, and it still is. It is the only institution in the black community that has as many people in one place at one time. Historically the black church functioned as the social catalyst for black folk; racism in American society did not allow black people to function in any other social context outside the church. For instance, if we wanted to have a fashion show, we could not put it on at the fashion salon downtown; we had to have our fashion shows in church. If we wanted to put on concerts, we could not rent the music hall or the local auditorium because we were not allowed as black people to have access to it; so we had to put our concerts on in church. We were not allowed to play politics in the broader political society, so we played politics in church. That is why some of us tend to chuckle when white people say black folk are not ready politically in our society — because we have been playing political games in our church denominational structures for centuries.

All you have to do is go to an AME, AME Zion, or National Baptist convention where black folk gather and where they're campaigning and candidating for bishop, moderator, and president to understand that black folks do understand political ramifications of interacting with people. It is interesting that the people who were perhaps the most ardent critics of the black church over the last decade have now begun to join the black church. More than half of the "Main 21," a group that directs one of the largest gang structures in Chicago, have joined strategic black churches in the Chicago area. Huey

Newton, the founder of the Black Panther party, has joined a black church because he recognizes the fact that the black church represents potentially the most strategic political, social organization in the black community and that anything that is going to be done with many hundreds and thousands of black people must be done through the black church.

While membership in many churches in the broader white community is declining, in the United States membership in the black community church is still going up. Young people are still going to church. The black church is here to stay for a while, whatever its problems and difficulties are.

The role that the black church must play in the black man's struggle against racism, his struggle for liberation and total equality, is to become a live model on earth of what is happening in heaven. This, of course, is the function of the whole Church as founded by Jesus Christ. The black church, therefore, must have a twofold purpose: it must be the voice of God, and it must be the force of God in the black community. It must be the body or community in the black neighborhood that is constantly giving God's point of view and God's perspective about any movement for liberation among black people. It must challenge black people to fight and struggle for liberation. It must be able to point out where the forces of darkness are. It must be able to call sin "sin." It must speak openly against the oppressor; but it must also deal with the sin and unrighteousness within its own community. It must make sure the people in the black community who are struggling for liberation understand that liberation is God's battle, that the liberation is God's objective, that it is not simply a civil rights struggle but a struggle of God. If the battle is going to be won, it must be won on God's terms.

The black church must call black people to both individual and social salvation. One great difficulty in church life in America has been that on one side we've had a group of people who are interested in saving people's souls by giving them a passport out of hell to heaven, but are not concerned about the social responsibility that goes with it. They are not concerned that people have to live with rats and roaches and slum landlords and police brutality and drug addiction and broken homes. On the other hand, there are our liberal friends who have been much concerned about saving the society corporately, and they talk about social salvation. But you cannot have a corporate society without having individuals to make up that corporate community, and thus there must be a gospel that communicates the need for man's personal liberation as well as corporate liberation in the community to which that individual belongs. The role of the black church, therefore, must be to seek to reconcile men with men, and men with God. The black church must emerge in the black community as a "new community," that is, a live model on earth of what is happening in heaven.

The black church must also become the moral leader of the nation at home. God has always used a previously or a contemporarily oppressed people to provide moral and spiritual leadership to their generation. Black people by virtue of their oppression, by virtue of the racism committed against them, have a greater sensitivity to righteousness and justice than the oppressor. This does not mean black people are more righteous, or more just, but they are more sensitive to justice. The taste buds of a person who has not eaten for several days tend to be more acute than those of a man who has been eating on a regular basis. The black church must be calling people to a relationship with God. It must call this community to righteousness, to a personal relationship with Jesus Christ by inviting the resurrected Christ to live in them. This new community, made up of oppressed people who are committed to Jesus Christ and who have been liberated by Him, are able to provide the moral leadership for a decaying society. To me the black church remains the only salvation, not only for black people, but for the white community as well.

Now, when I say the black church remains the only hope, I do not mean in its present form. I believe the black church needs to be revolutionized. It needs to be called back to the responsibility that it fulfilled in the black community until

150 years ago. It needs to be cleaned out in the sense that the false prophets among us must be driven out, the racketeers must be driven out, and those who do not have divine credence for their authority as preachers and those who do not truly belong to the new community because they don't belong to Jesus Christ must be weeded out. The black church must begin to deal with the question of just having anybody join simply to build an empire. We must be able to say to ourselves that if we build empires the way white people build church empires, then we have no relevancy at all. Our relevancy must consist of being diametrically opposed to the basis on which the white church has sought to establish its new community... devoid of God, devoid of divine inspiration, devoid of divine sanction, devoid of the authority of the Scriptures. This must not be the lot of the revolutionized black church.

The black church was the creation of black people who from day to day had to deal with the overwhelming, brutal, agonizing reality of white power. During slavery the black church was the only source of personal identity and of a sense of community for black people. The black church was the only institution the white man did not mess around with. The black church became the only community of black people where they could survive without committing suicide or without being annihilated in mind and spirit. The black church became the only community where black people could reject the white master's definition of black humanity and rebel against it. The black church became the home base for revolution. The black church became the means of transporting slaves during the underground railroad — independent black churches in the North became underground railroad stations at which points slaves could get help in getting established in the North or in Canada. The black church became the platform for abolitionists and for those people who needed a platform to preach freedom and equality.

White Christianity had suggested that the Gospel was concerned about the freedom of only the soul and not the body. It was the black church that gave them a more holistic view of man based on the Scriptures. While many of the hymns and spirituals were worldly in their content, this was done only to be commensurate in nature. Black preachers preached "a land flowing with milk and honey on the other side of Jordan where every day would be Sunday by and by." But you must look at this in the light of the ever-present dehumanizing reality of white power. White people, by the very nature of the system they had created, demolished the idea in black people's minds that they could find hope in this present world. This is why they sang songs like, "Going Home on the Chariot in the Morning," "I'se So Glad Trouble Don't Last Always," "I Know the Otter World Is Not Like This." The black church never accepted the view of the white preacher that God ordained slavery for the black folk and that God had relegated black people to conditions of servitude. And generally, when slaves sang about heaven, it was because they realized the futility of rebellion, not because they accepted slavery. At the same time they did not allow all their spirituals to be engulfed in the other world. They also recognized that God is a God of liberation, so they sang songs like, "If God Delivered Daniel, Why Not Us?" or "When Israel Was in Egypt's Land, Let My People Go" — "'pressed so hard they could not stand, Let my people go. Go down Moses, way down in Egypt's land, tell old Pharaoh, let my people go." Even more aggressive was the spiritual, "Ole freedom, ole freedom over, me, 'fore I'd be a slave, I'd be buried in my grave and go home to my Lord and be free."

The black church must recapture this historic commitment. It must, for black people, become the House of Bread because it is built upon the Bread of Life, which is Jesus Christ, resurrected and alive from the dead. The black church must move to becoming more like the New Testament Christian church in structure. Historically we have embodied all the power and authority in one man, namely the black preacher. Thus the black church has been lax in building perpetual leadership at all levels of its structure. The function of the pastor is to "equip the saints for the work of the ministry" (see Eph. 4), and the pastor must become the trainer of his people for them to get out in the nitty-gritty, day-to-day brawls of doing battle with the enemy, struggling for the liberation of black people's minds and spirits. If he is to do it alone, then the black church cannot stand. But if he is to develop and train leadership that will exist at every level in the community in the name of Jesus, then it will be relevant and will work.

The emergence of the new community — that is, a live model on earth of what is happening in heaven — is to be the role of the black church in the black man's struggle for liberation.

The function of the church as the new community presupposes that the people who are a part of this fellowship have checked out what is happening in heaven. Jesus Christ put His finger on it when He taught His disciples to pray. He said, "When you pray, say: . . . 'your will be done on earth as it is in heaven'" (Luke 11:2). The function of the church is to do the will of God on earth the way it is happening in heaven. So that if people in the system need a live model of what God is doing in heaven, all they should have to do is to look at those people who are members of the community called "the church."

The church is made up of people who have made Jesus Christ the Master and priority of their lives. To that extent they are called out of the system, whose priorities are materialism, war, jealousy, envy, pride, injustice, etc. The people who make up this new community are not simply a congregation who builds a steeple and a church wall and stained-glass windows and altar rails, but they are literally a community of people living in commitment to each other twenty-four hours a day, seven days a week. If what is happening in heaven is justice, then this new community called the church ought to be practicing justice. If what is happening in heaven is peace, it means the people who are members of this new community called the church are not warlike. If what is happening in heaven is the destruction of the works of the devil — and the Bible says that is why Jesus Christ came — then the people who belong to this called-out group ought to be actively engaged in destroying the works of the devil. The works of the devil are hunger, poverty, racism, war, militarism, etc. All of these acts, and all those institutionalized forms in the world's system, are contrary to the standards of a Holy God. The people who are members of this new community called the church will infiltrate the world's system. They will be athletes, businessmen, politicians, educators, sociologists, psychologists — not for the purpose of succeeding within those sociological structures — but for the purpose of being representatives of the kingdom of God to those institutions. The function of the people who belong to this new community is to be like salt; and the function of salt is that it creates thirst. The new community makes people thirsty for God; people of the church community are like salt, and the salt penetrates without losing its saltiness. And the function of these people is to penetrate the world's system, to penetrate this evil, immoral, unjust world and to be light in darkness, to be honey in bitterness, and to be live models of what is going on in heaven.

This new community practices making love to God. We call that "worship." Worship is looking at Jesus Christ, looking at God, and saying: Wow! Out of sight! It's grooving off of God. It's praising God. It's making love to Him. And this is what this new community does. It becomes obsessed with making love to God. Another function of this new community called the church is that it seeks to reconcile men to God. It calls men to commitment to Jesus Christ. It goes into this evil system and seeks to call people out of it. Now, this means that a person who is a member of this community called the church will be actively engaged in the destruction of this present system, not with guns, bullets, or bombs, nor with going out and creating physical war, because the Apostle Paul is very clear in Scripture that our weapons are not carnal. "For our struggle is not against flesh and blood, but against the rulers, against the authorities, against the powers of this dark world..." (Eph. 6:12). We do not use the weapons of the world, but we are engaged in destroying the world's system built on greed, materialism, war, envy, pride, and brokenness. We are seeking to bring men to God, who ultimately reconciles men to men. So the function of the church is to be the agent of reconciliation. We seek to reconcile men with God and men so that we build this new community.

Another function of the church is that it gives witness. It is a witnessing community. It witnesses to the power of God; it witnesses to the validity and authenticity of Jesus Christ; it witness, by its lifestyle, to the authority of the Scriptures' being God's Word; it witnesses to the resurrection of Jesus Christ. The greatest argument for the resurrection of Jesus Christ lies not so much in our ability to argue His resurrection in terms of its historical factuality or to argue it intellectually or rationally, but in that God is alive in Christ living out His lifestyle through His people called the church community. Again, please do not confuse what I call "the church," this new community, with what exists denominationally known as Presbyterian, Baptist, Methodist, or Episcopalian, etc. While there are people among them who are forging this new community and building it, they are not denominationally the new community. The new community is made up of those people who have trusted Jesus Christ, whose lives have been transformed, who have been reconciled to God, who are seeking to be live models on earth of what is happening in heaven.

One other function in this new community called the church is that it disciples people. And the word "disciple" has the root in it of the word "discipline." Essentially we are the disciples of Jesus Christ, which means we bring ourselves under the discipline of Jesus Christ as expressed in His Word. And the Word of God, the Scripture, becomes the constitution of this new community, becomes its bylaws. It becomes the blueprint of this new community. Some churches do a good job of reconciling men with God and bringing people to the experience of the new birth whereby they receive eternal life in Jesus Christ, but many churches do a very bad job in raising those kids once they have been born again. The church must function not only as a maternity ward, but also as a nursery that raises people. One of the most critical areas which people unwilling to be subject to the authority of Jesus Christ point to is the hypocrisy and the lack of maturity among the people who call themselves God's people. The only reply I can give to those people who are very critical of our behavior as Christians and our behavior as members of the new community is to ask them not to judge God by some of His retarded children. This in brief is the function of this new community called "the church."

What is the role of the black preacher?

IF THE BLACK church is the most powerful social institution in the black community, it makes sense that the black preacher would emerge as the most powerful individual in the black community. Where the black preacher needs to be must be summed up in the words of Rev. Nathaniel Hall, who wrote in 1827,

> The progress of emancipation is certain. It is certain because God has made of one blood all nations of men, and He who is said to be no respecter of persons has so decreed. Did I believe that it would always continue and that men to the end of time would be permitted with impunity to usurp the same undue authority on his fellows, I would ridicule the religion of the Saviour of the world. I would consider my Bible as a book of false and delusive fables and commit it to flame. Nay, I would still go further, I would at once confess myself an atheist, deny the existence of a holy God.

The role of a black preacher in terms of his methodology has always changed based on the times. During slave days some black preachers like the Rev. Hyland Garnet urged outright rebellion against the evils of white power. His estimation of the white man's mind was: to appeal to the white man on the basis of love and goodwill would have little effect because they were too warped. Therefore he taught that the spirit of liberty is a gift from God, and God thus endows the slaves with the zeal to break the chains of slavery. In one address, recorded in 1848 in Buffalo, New York, he said:

> If a band of Christians should attempt to enslave a race of heathen men and to entail slavery upon them and to keep them in heathenism in the midst of Christianity, the God of heaven would smile upon every effort which the injured might take or make to disenthrall themselves. Brethren, it is as wrong for your lordly oppressor to keep you in slavery as it was for the manthief to steal our ancestors from the coast of Africa. You should therefore, now use the same amount of resistance as would have been just in our ancestors when the bloody foot prints of the first thief were placed upon the shores of our father land. The humblest peasant is as free in the sight of God as the proudest monarch that ever swayed a scepter. Liberty is a spirit sent from God and is like its great author. It is no respecter of persons. Brethren, the time has come when you must act for yourself. It is an old and true saying, that if hereditary bondmen would be free they must themselves strike the blow.

Nat Turner, a slave rebel, was a Baptist preacher who led perhaps the most successful slave revolt in the history of the United States. Not only did he do this, but he felt commissioned by God to do so. And while it is true that most black preachers did not take part in revolts, few failed to see that God hates slavery.

Many white people sought to convince black people that the reason God permitted them to be slaves was because a curse was upon them and this was done to punish them for their sins. This put a great number of black people in what James Cone refers to as "existential absurdity." They could not understand why God permitted slavery. Like the biblical Job they knew whatever their sins or the sins of their forefathers, it did not justify slavery. The punishment did not fit the crime.

After slavery, during Reconstruction, many public positions were filled by black preachers. The program and direction of

The Role of the Black Church

the black community changed, but only for a short period of time, because when Reconstruction ended, the black preacher was openly removed from his public position. Consequently black people had to find new ways to relate to these new power structures. They found it difficult to relate to a society that declared them free but forced them to behave like slaves. Thus the black church during this period lost its zeal for freedom in the midst of these new structures for white power. The rise of segregation and racism in the post-Civil War period somewhat nullified the drive for equality. The black preacher remained the spokesman for black people. But he faced some tremendous difficulties because many of his fellows succumbed to the bribery of the white power structure in an attempt to negate his power as the preacher. His preaching changed from a drive for freedom, equality, and liberation to speaking against drinking, dancing, and smoking, which at that particular time was, and to a great extent still is, the hangup of a good number of white preachers.

The black preacher slackened his drive to deal with the freedom and struggle for liberation in the present world to to talk about the kingdom beyond this world. Many black churches began to adopt the theology of white missionaries and taught the blacks to forget the present and look to the future. Some black ministers even urged blacks to adopt the morality of white society. The black preacher began to suggest that any black person who was arrested by the police or put into prison was an immoral person, simply because the white society decreed him to be so. I think, though, that because of the bribery and because of the selling-out of many black preachers to the white power structure during the late 1920s and '30s, tremendous criticism began to come out of the black as well as the white community against the black preacher. Some of these criticisms were — and I quote:

> — Blood suckers! They'll take the food out of your mouth and make you think they're doing you a favor. You take these preachers — they're living like kings! They got great big Packard automobiles and ten or twelve suits and

a bunch of sisters putting food in their pantry. Do you call that religion? Naw, it ain't nothin' but a bunch of monkey foolishness.

— I'm a church member. I believe churches are still useful. But like everything else, there's a lot of racketeering going on in the church.

— Ministers are not so conscientious as they used to be. They're money-mad nowadays. All they want is the Almighty Dollar. That's all they talk about.

— The preachers want to line their pockets with gold. They're supposed to be the leaders of a people, but they are fake leaders.

It must be pointed out that many black preachers committed apostasy partly because had they not supported the caste system of segregation and discrimination, they would have placed their lives and the lives of their people in danger. They would have been lynched and their churches burned. Thus by co-operating with the system they protected their lives and the lives of their people from the menacing threat of white racism. Now this is not an excuse for their lack of obedience to Christ — it merely explains it.

In the words of James Cone,

> The real sin of the black church and its leaders is that they even convince themselves that they are doing the right thing by advocating obedience to white oppression as a means of entering, at death, the future age of heavenly bliss. The black church identified white words with God's word and convinced its people that by listening, in faithful obedience, to the great white father they would surely enter the pearly gates. Thus, the creativity of the black church which characterized the pre-Civil War period is missing after the war.

The role of a black preacher today is that he must be the general of the forces of God in the black community as well as in the broader white community. The black preacher must stand on the prophetic wall and be as open as he has been historically to all the things that will be thrown at him. The black preacher needs to be the embodiment of the live model of what the new community called the church is really all about. He should, in fact, be the suffering servant. He must be an example of what the new community is preaching about, and he must be the instrument of God in rallying people to become part of that new community, the church. The role of the black preacher is to be a proclaimer. He must be a proclaimer to the people in the new community of what they ought to be, of what's going on in heaven. His proclamation must not only come from the pulpit of the church structure, but also come from out where the people are. He must be rubbing shoulders with the people. His words must come like a two-edged sword because they are the words of God. He must speak the Word of God. He must speak in the tradition of the prophet, and his message must be so straight, so honest, so cutting, and so sharp that he will also reap the kind of response from people that was reaped by the prophets. He must be prepared to die because he is telling the truth. He must realize that when he stands up and proclaims the truth, he is going to become the target of a racist society that seeks to ridicule him. He will be called Communist-inspired. He will be called militant. He will be called a revolutionist. He will be called an anarchist. He will be called a left-winger because he speaks the truth against a racist, demonic society. But he is also going to get it from his own people. He will get it from them because he is rubbing shoulders with them. He must be out there where black folks are struggling for better housing, better educational opportunities, where they're struggling for employment just to make a decent living. He must be out there telling them that while bread is important, the Bread of Life is equally if not more important.

This is going to be difficult. It is going to be difficult to stand up and talk to people while struggling with them for housing, employment, and education, then to also let them know that unless they become part of the new community they will never be able to get the things rightly. They will get them, but they will not get them rightly unless they become part of the community Jesus has come to establish. He's got to stand up and proclaim to black people that if they get what they want the way white folk have got it, they are thieves and robbers...theirs will not be the kingdom.

And he must preach this no matter how unpopular he becomes. He will be called a thief and a hustler by white folk. He will be called an Uncle Tom by black folk and he must be all that in order to be the suffering servant. He must not rebel at being called all those names because that is the role of the black preacher. He must stand up and proclaim to black people that if they are seeking bread in any other place but the bread house, they are thieves and robbers. And he must preach that. He must proclaim to black folk that there cannot be new people without a relationship to God as expressed in the resurrection of His Son, Jesus Christ. Wherever he goes, he's got to hold that line. He's going to be in some meetings where black professionals discuss the sociology or the psychology of the "movement," and while there he must do one thing — proclaim the Word of God. He must interject it, he must affirm it, he must proclaim it. He must do so even at the disappointment of other people because that is the role of the black preacher.

Tom, in your book Black and Free *you were very hard on the black preacher. Have you met with any difficulty because of this?*

LET ME SAY that I was not hard on the black preacher to the extent that I felt the immorality and unrighteousness I described as existing among some black clergymen is more prevalent than that among white clergymen. This is not the case. In fact, since there are more white clergymen than black clergymen, this would be a more rampant problem among whites. But I am tougher on the black preacher because the black preacher is the head of the most powerful social institution in the black community—the black church. And I'm also hard on him because to whom much is given much is required. The moral leadership for this country is going to have to come from black people, because oppressed people always have a greater sensitivity to righteousness and justice than the oppressor. It is not by accident that God has always chosen a previously or contemporarily oppressed people to bring moral judgment on a nation or a generation. This does not mean black people are more righteous or more moral, but because of our oppression we are more sensitive to righteousness and morality. And since this morality must come from black people, and the black church must become the catalyst for producing moral leadership in the black community and in America in general, then the black preacher has a greater responsibility. One of my roles is to challenge him to that responsibility and to challenge those who are committed to moral standards and to be difficult with those who are giving the rest of us a bad name.

BLACK THEOLOGY

What is black theology? Why is it necessary?

"BLACK THEOLOGY" created the same kind of response in many people as did the term "black power." Right away people believed that black theology was developing a separate view of God, that we were breaking Him up into a white God and a black God, that the development of a black theology presupposed a white theology, and this in their minds produced a dichotomy. But let's look at the literal definition of the word "theology," which means the study of God. If theology is the study of God, when we talk about black theology we are talking about a study of God through the black experience. Thus we're not necessarily talking about a separate theology. As it is, we're talking about looking at God through the eyes of the black experience which is a unique experience for the white society.

To that extent, all cultures have a theology. You could say there is an Indian theology or a Chinese theology, etc. It doesn't mean that there are separate answers, or that the Bible gets broken up into the cultural idiosyncrasies of the world, but rather that these people do have a way of viewing God from where they are. Black people's heritage comes up out of Africa; out of 250 years of slavery in this country; out of 100 years of struggle since slavery to have our God-given right to determine our own futures. It comes up out of the experience of being on the bottom of the economic, social, political ladder in American society. It comes up out of the experience of being oppressed and not having access to the system. Thus we have a different perspective about God than the oppressor does. Thus the need for a black theology.

For instance, look at some of the people who were critics of the Old Testament. Some of them were subsequently labeled by Church Fathers as heretics. One can understand this, when one looks at the critics of the Old Testament in light of the Hebrew scholars and the people through whom the New Testament was written as inspired by God. The Hebrews had a far different perspective of God than the theological critics did. Of course, the theological critics were looking at God from where they sat. They were looking at Him from their ivory towers of scholarliness and intellectualism, whereas the Hebrews were looking at God from their struggle from slavery and depression — a God who brought them up out of Egypt and a God who delivered them through the Red Sea. So naturally their perspective about God was different. My suggestion is that black folk's experience with God would be slightly different from their oppressors'. Thus we need to study God in the light of the black people's experience. Someone else has said the study of theology is giving biblical answers to questions currently being asked. I suggest the questions being asked in the black community today are different from the questions being raised in the typical middle-class white society. We need to know what God's answers are to the questions black folk are raising out of the black experience.

It is important, when we deal with the question of black theology, that we do not get hung up on the word "black." It is not limited simply to the skin condition of a man. Black theology is a theology basically to deal with the questions raised by all oppressed people. It was not by accident that whenever God wanted to speak to a generation, He always used a previously or presently oppressed people to do so, because oppressed people have a greater sensitivity to righteousness and justice than the oppressor. This does not mean oppressed people are more righteous; rather, they have a greater sensitivity. The taste buds of a man who has not eaten for several days tend to be a bit more acute than those of the man who has been eating on a regular basis. As God chose the Israelites to speak to their generation, as God used Germans to bring about the Reformation, as God has used any particular people who are available to Him at a particular time, God is also at this juncture of history speaking through black people, prophesying to the American society through black men and women who belong to Him.

It could be said by any social analyst that the theology of Jesus was Hebrew theology, or that the theology of the prophets like Jonah, Ezekiel, and Daniel was Hebrew theology. What it simply meant was, God chose to reveal Himself through Hebrew people. But the Bible makes it very plain that while He entered into a covenant with Jacob and changed Jacob's name to Israel, all people who were willing to meet the conditions of that covenant — be they Moabites or Amalekites or Canaanites — would reap the same benefits of the covenant that Jacob reaped. They would have their names changed, and they would reap the benefits of the new covenant because they had entered into a relationship with God. "Never forget that once you were heathen, and that you were called godless and 'unclean' by the Jews. (But their hearts, too, were still unclean, even though they were going through the ceremonies and rituals of the godly, for they circumcised themselves as a sign of godliness.) Remember that in those days you were living utterly apart from Christ; you were enemies of God's children and He had promised you no help. You were lost, without God, without hope. But now you belong to Christ Jesus, and though you once were far away from God, now you have been brought very near to Him because of what Jesus Christ has done for you with His blood" (Eph. 2:11-13 *The Living Bible*).

We're saying that God today, to a great extent, is speaking through an oppressed people who are committed to Him. Thus what they say takes on the flavor of their experience — in the case of black folk, the black experience. This does not mean the message is exclusively to black people; all folk who are willing to hear the message of God to oppressed people, and who are willing to enter into the covenant God has provided in His Son Jesus Christ, become part of this new community God is building on earth called the kingdom of God.

Black theology does say, though, that the faith has been contaminated with and prostituted by secularism and by people with warped thinking; a lot of this warped thinking has been perpetuated in white racism. Black theology is an attempt to strip the New Testament and to strip Jesus of the adverse cultural trappings that have been placed on Him and that have been used to oppress people further.

Black theology, therefore, is an attempt to save Jesus from Christianity. It is an attempt to show black people that a commitment to Jesus Christ is not a commitment to a docile, subjective kind of Christ, but rather to a gutsy, contemporary, radical revolutionary. It is an attempt to say that the gospel of Jesus Christ is about the liberation of the oppressed; that the gospel of Jesus Christ is about setting people free; that the gospel of Jesus Christ is about saturating the common clay of a man's humanity with the lifestyle of Jesus; that the gospel of Jesus Christ is about feeding hungry people and putting clothing on naked people's backs. Black theology has as its task to analyze the black man's condition in light of God's revelation in Jesus Christ with the purpose of creating a new black humanity among black people; of providing the necessary substance in that people to destroy oppression, poverty, hunger, racism, and war — in fact, to destroy all the works of the devil.

Like any theology, black theology must have a frame of reference. It is here that there will be division among black theologians. There are some black theologians who seek to make their frame of reference purely the black experience, but this assumes the black experience is absolutely moral and absolutely just, and that is not the case. There must be a moral frame of reference through which the black experience can be judged; the validity of the black experience, in the eyes of God, must stand up under the moral frame of reference. It is to this point that I accept the statement presented by a group of free churchmen to the archbishop of Canterbury regarding the authority of the Protestant tradition. These churchmen said, "Ultimate and absolute authority in the matter of faith can and must reside only in the Word of God, who was made flesh in Christ, died and rose again for our salvation, and abides forever in His church. In Him and through Him, God has spoken to men. Here only have we the unmistakable voice of God unimpeded in utterance by the weakness of sinful nature and the fallibility of sinful human thought." As it was for Luther it must also be for me and for all sincere black theologians: Christ alone is supreme authority, and the Scriptures are second only to Christ.

On the question of eschatology, black theology rejects simply telling black people to look to the future. "I got a robe, you got a robe, all of God's children got a robe." Or we were taught, "Take this old world but give me Jesus." What really happened was, I took Jesus and the white man took the world. Black theology says that if our eschatology says Jesus Christ is ushering in a new heaven and a new earth, then our Christology says that with our two feet planted on the earth we have to be working to bring about that new community now; that we are on earth on the way to heaven; that we reject the other-worldly point of view which says simply, "Since we're all going to heaven, let us not concern ourselves with food, clothing, poverty, shelter, hunger, war, and racism, which are nonsense and totally contrary to the Scriptures and totally separate from the tradition of the prophets.

Do you advocate that black people unite behind one religion in order to accomplish their liberation?

I'M NOT NAIVE enough to suffer from illusions that black people will unite behind any one thing. Black people have such diverse personalities and such differences of opinion politically, economically, sociologically, and educationally that it will not be possible to get all 25 million people committed to one political ideology or one religion. I think realization of the inability to unite black people behind a single ideology came out of the first black political convention which met in Gary, Indiana, in March 1972. There was the difficulty of coming to any particular agreement on the methodology for the liberation of black people. Therefore, I don't believe that people are going to line up behind any single religion. But it is also important for you to understand that I am not in a religion bag. Religion is defined as that which a person feels to be of ultimate value and what action he takes in the light of it. So one can be a Communist, a Buddhist, a Methodist, Presbyterian, Pentecostal, Episcopalian, agnostic, or an atheist — and be religious. Whatever is of ultimate value to a person and whatever action he takes to fulfill that ultimate value — that is his religion. In that case, religions come a dime a dozen. I wouldn't cross the street to get you interested in religion, because I am interested in changing human nature. It is impossible to build a "new community" without fundamentally and radically transforming human nature.

There cannot be a new community without new people. This is a point the new revolutionaries miss. They assume that if you have enough idealistic people, all of them committed to changing the system and all of them committed to producing something new, then that is all you need. But, you see, simply having the theory of a new society will not produce a new society unless you have new people capable of practicing a new society — which leads us back to fundamentally changing people. We are all selfish, egotistical, manipulative, exploitive, oppressive, envious, jealous. We all have these characteristics in our nature which negate the possibility of our being committed to each other.

A few of the movements in the black community are trying to produce this new society. For instance, take the Black Muslims. Thirty to forty years ago they were a very radical group committed to bringing about transformation within the black community. They were talking about negating the white system and destroying it, burning it down, etc. But you don't hear that today. They preached a very radical message; out of that radicalism emerged perhaps the greatest evangelist among the Black Muslims, Malcolm X. But the Black Muslim movement today is no longer a radical organization. They are a conservative organization because they've accumulated millions of dollars worth of property. They own thousands of acres of farmland. They own their own stores. They have abolished the middle man. They're selling to themselves. They own hotels, apartment buildings, and schools, so essentially they have become part of the system. These people who were yesterday radical are today conservative, because yesterday's radical must become today's conservative. He has to become conservative in order to conserve what he had accumulated when he was radical.

Now there's developing within the Black Muslim movement an internal struggle for power. As the Honorable Elijah Muhammad gets older and death approaches, there is that internal struggle over who will control the empire. Part of the reason Malcolm X was suspended from the Black Muslim movement prior to his assassination, was that there were people who were the gate keepers of the Honorable Elijah Muhammad who felt Malcolm was becoming too powerful. As a result, today Black Muslims are ripping each other off in the streets, killing each other, negating each other, because they have not dealt fundamentally with the egotism, selfishness, jealousies, and lust for power that are in all human beings.

Take another radical movement in the middle and upper class white society, known as SDS — Students for Democratic Society. Seven years ago they perhaps were the most radical group on college and university campuses. They were doing a good job in the sense that they were analyzing what the issues were. Their diagnoses were not always accurate because they did not come to grips with the fundamental problems of human nature. So these kids marched and demonstrated, burned administration buildings, tied and gagged college presidents, cut the phone lines, disrupted classrooms on campus, robbed many students of the opportunity to continue their education, in the name of producing a democratic society. Today SDS has broken up into nine splinter groups. Over what? Over personality differences, over struggle for power, over who will be chief...all the problems the system they are trying to fight against is bound up with. In other words, they are victims of the very sin they were trying to deal with. It brings us back to—you have got to deal with human nature.

Another example would be the Black Panther movement in the black community. Again, the Black Panthers began to stir up a great sense of pride in nationalism among black people, which was good. And they were beginning to teach black people that they needed to form coalitions within their own community and not simply be the lackeys of the white political machine downtown. That was good. They discovered the hundreds of black young people who don't eat decent breakfasts in the morning, and so they started having these special breakfast programs. They began to feed hundreds of children, which was good. But now the Black Panther movement is splintered, broken. For all intents and purposes it is dead. Black Panthers are killing each other, shooting each other on the street, because nobody dealt with the problem of human nature, the lust for power, envy, greed, selfishness.

That is why I am into Jesus—because there has to be some frame of reference, some moral lifestyle, that can make the difference in my life, that will negate my attempt to exploit and oppress, and that will give me the kind of security I need. I don't need personal power only, but the kind of power to build the kind of community that God intended man to have. The person who is following Jesus Christ does not need credit. He does not need to be in the limelight; he does not need to be applauded. Therefore, if we are going to have a true liberation movement it has to be led by and made up of people who've had their human natures fundamentally transformed, who've adopted the Jesus lifestyle, who've operated from a position of security so that they can say to our people: "Look, I don't want anything from you, I don't need to be applauded by you, I don't need to be a name among you, I'm not interested in money, wealth, fame, or fortune. You tell me what it is that you're seeking that is commensurate with the kingdom of God, that fulfills all that God intended man to be, and I will bring all the resources at my disposal to help you achieve it. Let anyone take the credit. I'm just interested in seeing the job done." Now, that is the true point of view of people who are true followers of Jesus.

Are you suggesting that Jesus Christ should be the unifying force for all black people?

AGAIN, I'M NOT that naive to believe that all black people are going to buy Jesus. What I am saying is, black people — like all people — need something to deal with the basic problem of human nature. At this point I run into a problem, because what I'm saying sounds superpietistic. We live in a society where people are trying to bring about a collective liberation, or corporate liberation, and don't feel we have time to get into this individual pietistic bag of personal transformation through (some kind of) religious conversion. But while I'm committed to corporate liberation, and while I'm committed to the liberation of black people (in the sense that we need to have the right to determine our own futures and the power to determine and direct those political, social, and economical institutions that affect our destiny), I do not believe you can produce a corporate society without producing individuals capable of making up that corporate society. These individuals, if they are not new people, will not produce a new corporate community. Pietistic or not, there has to be a certain kind of individual commitment in order to bring about a collective movement.

If a group of us get together and decide we want a particular candidate to represent us, enough of us as individuals have got to be convinced we have to vote for that cat, and we must individually go down to the polls and vote. Then when we tally up the votes we can say that the blacks in the community voted for that candidate, but they were individuals in the black community who went and voted, and those individuals made up the corporate community. If you are going to have a new community, you have got to have new people. Now, all black people are not going to buy this, any more than all white people will. But I'm saying that those who are interested in being live models of the new community need to have this personal transformation.

An example of what I'm talking about is the book *Black Power* authored by Stokely Carmichael and Charles Hamilton. In that book they were asked the question, "What guarantee is there, if black people assume power over their institutions and are able to control their own futures, that they will act any different from white people?" The authors' answer was, "Human nature being what it is, there is no guarantee." And they're right. So, how do we change human nature? Again that brings us back to Jesus Christ, who said, "I am the way, the truth, and the life." It was the Apostle Paul who said of Jesus Christ in 2 Corinthians 5:17, "Therefore if any man be in Christ, he is a new creature: old things are passed away; behold, all things are become new" (KJV). To have a new community you have to have new people.

If you are into some other bag — if you have discovered some other catalyst whereby people can get it together and form this new community that will have justice, mercy, love, kindness, goodness, self-control, and peace — and you can do this without Jesus Christ, I say, "Power to you!" But for me, Jesus Christ has proven historically, contemporarily, and in terms of the evidence experimentally as well as objectively, to be the only person I know capable of putting individuals together into a corporate community who can be live models of what God intended the community to be.

CHURCH AND STATE

*Y*ou stated that one of the functions of the new community
is to destroy the works of the devil and that those who are
members of the new community are actively engaged in the
destruction of this present world's system. To what extent
should the church react against society at large or against the
laws of government of its country? Doesn't Romans 13 tell us
we should be subject to the higher authorities because they
are ordained of God?

PERHAPS ONE OF the Scriptures used constantly by politically conservative people who claim to be followers of Jesus
Christ, but at the same time want to preserve the present
system, is to fall back on Romans 13. And they tend to quote
and interpret that Scripture out of context. The Scripture
reads we should be subject to the higher authorities because
they are ordained of God. That means simply that all authority
is ordained of God because God has put laws and authority
in His universe.

If you look at the Church as structured in the New Testament (it is to be a live model on earth of what is happening in
heaven), you will see that God invested people with authority.
Some pastors, some teachers, some administrators, many with
gifts, some with the gift of the evangelist, gift of helps, etc.
And there was authority that went with these positions of
gifts. The position of a father — that is, a person who has children — has authority as a father. God has given certain authority to a father. God has given certain authority to a mother.
It does not mean everything a father does is ordained of God,
simply because his authority is ordained of God. And not
everything a mother does is ordained of God, although her
authority is ordained of God. The position of senator or con-

Church and State   121

gressman or city councilman or state legislator is a position of authority which is ordained by God. But not everything a legislator or congressman or senator does in that office is ordained by God. The authority in the office of the president of the United States is ordained of God, but not everything the president does in authority is ordained of God.

The function of us who are members of the new community is to watch people like presidents and congressmen and senators and legislators; whenever they act in authority contrary to the Word of God, we must prophesy against them. We must resist them. And because we resist them when they act contrary to the Word of God does not mean we do not respect them or mean we are anarchist or Communist. It simply means we, at this point, are invoking our subjection to the higher government, which is the kingdom of God. If you're going to call people anarchist or label them as committing acts of treason simply because they resist authorities who act contrary to the Scriptures and the standards of God, then you would also have to do the same thing for the apostles. You have precedent for this in Acts 4, when Peter and John were arrested and told never again to teach or preach in the name of Jesus. In verses 19 and 20 Peter and John answered and said to the Sanhedrin, which was the highest council of authority among the Jews: "Judge for yourselves whether it is right in God's sight to obey you rather than God. For we cannot help speaking about what we have seen and heard" (NIV). There are numerous occasions, especially in the Book of Acts, in which the disciples were arrested and told that if they were ever caught preaching Jesus again, they would be put to death. And the moment they were let go — the moment the authorities released them — they went back to the same spot where they had been arrested and started preaching again because they had made it clear it was right. You must judge whether it is right to listen to men rather than to God. The answer is obvious — you have to listen to God.

It was the same situation Martin Luther faced during the Reformation days when he knew he was rebelling against established authority. But what he saw in the Scriptures and what he saw in the practice of those people in authority did not match. They were not parallel; they were not integrated. So he said, "Here I stand, and I can do no other." I believe the day is now here in America when those of us who will be disciplined by the authority and the lordship of Jesus Christ must be prepared to die, go to jail, or be ostracized in the broader community for doing God's thing — which will be in violation of man's thing, which takes shape in institutional and governmental form.

Tom, doesn't this go contrary to the history of America? Isn't America a God-fearing nation? Wasn't our country founded by God-fearing people, thus eliminating any need to rebel against it?

AGAIN, LET ME make this very clear. I'm not talking about rebellion for rebellion's sake. I am not an anarchist. Neither do I advocate anarchy. But when the governments of this world act in direct contradiction to the Word of God, I must resist those governments.

In answer to your questions: America was not founded by God-fearing people. There were people among the early settlers who were God-fearing, who were committed to the lordship and the authority of Jesus Christ. We must also make a distinction between the Puritans who landed at Plymouth Rock in 1620 or 1621 and those people who constitutionally founded this country 150 years later. They were not the same crowd.

Some people say, "But our country *was* founded by God-fearing people! George Washington prayed at Valley Forge; Ben Franklin opened the first Congress in prayer." Yet all these people have to do is sit down and read the theology of

George Washington or Ben Franklin. Both of them were deists. Neither one believed in personal transformation through Jesus Christ or the building of a corporate community known as the Church who would be live models on earth of what is happening in heaven. They were not committed to the redemptive work of Jesus Christ on the cross; they did not believe that His shed blood provides reconciliation between God and man and that Christ arose from the dead to live His life through the humanity of any person who trusts Him. Ben Franklin, in fact, was fond of the phrase, "Variety is the spice of life" — and he left enough illegitimate children in Paris to prove it.

I will grant to you that there was a Christian witness in America. The first hundred or so colleges and universities established in America were established for the purpose of preparing people for the defense of the Gospel ministry. If you look at the constitutions or their preambles of such Ivy League and colonial schools as Princeton, Harvard, Yale, and William and Mary, you will see that all were founded for the purpose of giving people an education to prepare them to communicate the claims of Jesus Christ in society. It is interesting, though, that in the present age it is difficult even to mention the name Jesus on those campuses without risking ridicule, but at least that is what they were founded for. So to suggest that America is a God-fearing nation and was founded by God-fearing people would be ludicrous. It is because of this insanity that there are many superpatriotic, religious Americans running around with Bibles in one hand and American flags in the other. They have taken God, wrapped Him up in the American flag, and made Him president of the New York Stock Exchange, chairman of the Republican Party, head of the Joint Chiefs of Staff, super-capitalist extraordinary, and founder of the American system. They even put bumper stickers on their cars saying SUPPORT GOD AND COUNTRY as if they go together.

If God and America go together, then it also makes God the enemy. It means God founded a country in which He institutionalized slavery. It means that God is responsible for

Church and State

killing thousands of Africans who were shipped here during slave days and died along the way; that God was responsible for the brutalization and massacre of thousands of Indians and forcing the few Indians left in this country to live in isolated pockets called reservations; that God is responsible for the oppression of Chicanos; that God is responsible for the lack of social upward mobility of twenty-five million black people, five million Chicanos, and assorted other groups oppressed in our society. One percent of the population of America has 43 percent of all the dollars, 1 percent of the population has 39 percent of all the common stock invested in the major corporations in America, 1 percent of all the businesses in America makes 70 percent of all the profits — and if God and America go together, it means God has decided to concentrate all the wealth, power, and affluence into the hands of a small group of elitists because He is essentially an elitist God. Simply because we have stuck God's name on the money — "In God We Trust" — and simply because we have put Him into the salute to the American flag — "one nation under God" — does not make the statements true. America does not trust in God — it trusts in missiles, guns, bullets, war, oil wells, cars, and industry.

This nation is not under God. God doesn't run this country, He doesn't run our government, He doesn't run the state legislatures, the Congress, or the United States Senate. He doesn't run most of our homes. God doesn't even run some of our churches in America. It is historically inaccurate, as well as irrational, to believe that God ever has run or is now running America, or any system. One of the functions of the new community called the Church is to stand atop the wall and declare this: God is not an American anymore than He is a Russian or an Englishman or a German or a Frenchman. God is not a leftwinger or a rightwinger, He is not a conservative or a liberal, He is not an integrationist or a segregationist, He's not a capitalist or a Communist or a socialist. Jesus Christ is the Lord of heaven and earth and has come to establish His own thing. And His thing is not like anything that exists.

I suppose this point is summed up beautifully in the situation in Scripture in which Joshua is mapping out the battle of Jericho (Josh. 5:13-15). While he is viewing the city and planning the strategy, he notices a man standing off to his side with his sword unsheathed, dressed in full military regalia. Joshua observes that whichever side that man fights on will win the battle. So Joshua decides to check the man out. And he asks him a double question: "Do you fight with them, or do you fight with us?" And the man's answer was, "No, but as the captain of the Lord's host have I come." Joshua had asked the man a double question and the man gave him one No for both parts. In other words, the man said, in effect: "Joshua, I have not come to take sides. I've come to establish a whole new thing which I am in complete control of." At present, Jesus Christ is not in charge of this world's system. The Bible says, "The kingdoms of this world shall become the kingdom of our Lord and of His Christ and He shall reign for ever and ever" (see Rev. 11:15). The kingdoms of this world shall become...they are not now.

The function of the members of the new community who are committed to Jesus Christ is to become fifth columnists in the world's system for the purpose of subverting it in Jesus' name and calling people to repentance and reconciliation with God. They ought to be establishing on earth the kingdom, bringing as much of the domain of this present world out of Satan's control into the control of the lordship of Jesus Christ. The function of the Church is to help to bring about the kingdom of God on earth.

Now, at this point many people have difficulty because they believe the second coming of Jesus Christ is a sudden appearing whereby He will move into an evil world and establish a righteous kingdom. But if my eschatology says Jesus Christ is going to be bringing about a new heaven and a new earth, my Christology says I must be at work seeking to make that happen — not just sitting around merely saying the world is going to get worse and worse and twiddling my thumbs until He comes. I am to be a fifth columnist in the world's system for the purpose of subverting it and attracting people from it into the kingdom of God — and America is not the kingdom.

How do you deal with the issue of the separation of church and state?

I THINK THERE is no issue in American society that is more confusing, and on which people are less informed, than the separation of church and state. Much of the confusion has arisen from the Supreme Court's decision about prayer in the schools. If one reads the decision carefully, what the Supreme Court opposed was a state's prescribing prayer for students. For instance, the case that created the decision was where the teacher in the classroom had written out a specific prayer for the class to recite at the beginning of each day. Since that teacher is employed by the state, the Supreme Court ruled it would be unconstitutional for the teacher to prescribe a prayer for the students since the state in effect is thus doing it. Immediately people panicked and felt it meant we are to abolish all prayer from the schools. There is nothing that prohibits the teacher from allowing the students to recite their own prayers, or allowing them in the classroom to pray as they feel led. The constitutionality must be challenged for the impropriety of prescribing prayer by a state employee. There is nothing, for instance, that prohibits a teacher from reading the Scriptures in the classroom on a daily basis. Since the Bible speaks clearly for itself, especially with the new modern English translations of the Scripture, the Word of God can be communicated without one necessarily having to interpret what one reads. And since the Bible is accepted as good literature like Shakespeare or anybody else, the constitutional right to read the Scripture is guaranteed.

Nothing in the Constitution of the United States denies an

atheist the right to explain his atheistic ideas in class. Nothing stops a person who is opposed to the Bible from speaking in opposition to the Scriptures in the classroom. If that is the case, there is nothing to stop a person from giving a clear presentation of the historical accuracy of the Scripture or defending it as being the Word of God. Thus, when the Constitution deals with the separation of church and state, we are talking about separating or denying or prohibiting any particular religious denomination or religious group or religious organization from controlling the state or the government.

Since we live in a society where people hold to diverse religious beliefs, no state can therefore prescribe what people ought to believe. Nothing says that what people believe cannot have impact and influence on the state; so that while we are opposed to a state religion, there is nothing that prohibits a religious state. Nothing says people in positions of leadership and power cannot be people committed to the lordship and authority of Jesus Christ. I sincerely believe there ought to be people who understand the authenticity of the lordship of the Lord Jesus Christ putting others like them into positions of influence and decision-making power. Now, I'm not simply talking about people who are merely professing Christians and have even accepted Jesus Christ as their personal Savior, but have not received Him as Lord. They are not living under His authority and lordship, and thus they do not bring to their positions of authority the wide perspective of the kingdom of God. We have many people in positions of power and influence in this country who claim to be committed to Jesus Christ, yet advocate bombing people, advocate racism, advocate by their actions and decisions the continuation of oppression.

Indicative of what I am talking about, of how an evil system can continually be perpetuated even by religious folk, is the case in which one man, a lieutenant, goes out and massacres a whole village, killing some twenty-three people. He is brought to trial by a group of his peers, and yet the President of the United States, who is a religious man, decides to allow him to go free under full review of his case. At the same time there

Church and State

are two priests, the Berrigan brothers, whose crime is pouring duck's blood on Pentagon records — and they cannot go free. I wonder which is more immoral, the pouring of duck's blood on Pentagon records, or even the conspiracy to kidnap a high official of the United States, or a man who goes out and kills twenty-three people. I say there is something wrong with the values and priorities of even some of the religious people in power in this country, because they have not brought their religion under the lordship of the Lord Jesus Christ, and therefore they do not represent God's point of view on questions and issues of morality.

If one practices a consistent Christian lifestyle, he will become "illegal" in today's society. This country, even now, has begun to move against people who stand up and speak the truth. Why do you think the FBI tapped the telephone lines of Martin Luther King? They considered him "illegal." He was speaking out against the war long before it became popular, back in 1962 and '63. He stood up against injustice in the society, so he had to be investigated by the FBI and have his wires tapped. He was considered "illegal" because he was speaking the truth and trying to destroy some of the evil in the kind of system in which we live. It was for this reason the late J. Edgar Hoover called Martin Luther King "America's biggest liar." It was for this reason the rumor was put out that he was Communist-inspired. It was for this reason people put up posters around the country saying Martin Luther King was found one time lecturing to a group of card-carrying Communists which proved that he was Communist. These kinds of unjust things were brought against him in order to negate the truth he was speaking. The system was opposed to people who stood up and spoke the truth. You must consider that truth is an aspect of the kingdom of God because all truth is God's truth, no matter who says it.

Another classic example was the Attica prison situation that took place several years ago. When federal troops stormed Attica prison and several of the guards and inmates were killed, the word came out that the guards who were killed had

had their throats slit by the inmates. Yet the autopsy reports showed that the guards or the hostages were killed by the bullets of the invading troops. Under normal circumstances, the autopsy report would have been filed and kept quiet. But in this instance a young pathologist was in charge. Instead of sending his autopsy report through the channels, he called his own press conference and announced that the hostages had not been killed by inmates, but rather by the bullets of the troops. Shortly after this report was issued, all kinds of rumors began to spring up about this young pathologist that were aimed at discrediting his report. Some persons began to say that the young pathologist, when he was in medical school, cheated on his exam — thus bringing his honesty into question. Someone else tried to undermine the young man's integrity by saying he was separated and divorced from his wife as a woman-beater. Later it was disclosed he had never even married. All kinds of questions were raised about his competency as a medical officer.

You see, the problem in our society is that the moment a man issues a statement of truth that is contrary to the system and shows how oppressive and brutal the system is, we must find some way to discredit that truth. That is the nature of the system. Now, can you imagine — if that was what we would do with people who do not know Jesus Christ, but who speak the truth — what will happen when you as a Christian not only speak the truth, but live the truth and your entire life cuts across the grain of the system?

You have commented about a society that has engrossed itself in the Christian culture. What about those systems which reject the Christian culture, such as Communism?

THAT QUESTION assumes that capitalism is based on God,

and thus you would probably have to raise the converse question, "What do we do about cultures like Communism which are not based on God?" You do the same thing you do with cultures like capitalism which are not based on God. Capitalism and Communism are not essentially cultures, but rather political or economic forms, which, of course, are connected to cultures.

But aren't people in the Communist culture told not to believe in God?

YES, BUT THAT is also true under capitalism. Every time a company says profit is more important than anything else, they are saying there is no God. When people ask you to go out and serve the industrial complex and to make the company the biggest priority in your life, they are saying there is no God. Much of this has to do with how you hear and how you listen. The Communists get up and verbalize that there is no God. In capitalism we don't get up and verbalize it, but we say it anyway by our actions and our priorities. We have allowed industry to pollute the water and to pollute the air in the name of the extra dollar, and by polluting God's air and God's water we are saying there is no God. Automobile companies can produce cars today that will not pollute the air. We even have proof that cars can be manufactured to run on water and steam, and be run quite profitably, but the automobile companies are not allowed to do that. In fact, they are not about to do that because it will cut into their profit margins; so they go on making cars that emit fumes that pollute the air you and I have to breathe. They are in essence saying there is no God.

You must not be deluded that simply because we salute a flag in this country with a pledge that says, "One nation under

God," it is necessarily true. God has not run this country, does not now, and never will in the forseeable future. Because we've got God's name on our money, "In God We Trust," does not mean anything either.

Do you believe that Communism and its influence are in great part responsible for most of the unrest in the United States and Canada? And are Communists using the Negro situation to arrive at Communist ends?

I SUPPOSE the Communists in the United States sit down every now and then and chuckle at or at least take great pride in all the things they have been given credit for. There are some of us who fear Communists under every rock; in almost every disturbance, every adversity that develops in our country, we find a way to prove that the Communists created it. Sometimes we're never willing to admit that it is simply a result of our stupidity, that the Communists just aren't that smart or that powerful or that big.

Moreover, there's no such thing as a "Negro situation" or the "Negro problem." There is a white problem in America, not a black problem. Black people were not brought here from Africa by themselves. Black people did not institute slavery in this country. Black people didn't lynch themselves, black people didn't create segregation, black people don't move out of their neighborhoods when others move in, black people are not creating the laws and the conditions in the society which oppress them. White people do that. The amazing part about it is that the white people who've been oppressing black people are not Communists — they're good old red-blooded, God-fearing, flag-waving, patriotic Americans. We must recognize the fact that black people have never been interested in Communism, have never committed themselves

132   *Church and State*

to Communism. This isn't to say there haven't been notable blacks in the past thirty years who joined the Communist party or have been card-carrying Communists. But they have been a very small minority within the black community and have never exercised any kind of power and influence. Black people have been too busy trying to survive to even know what Communism is. Black people are essentially politically conservative. Most black people have no intentions of trying to destroy the United States or to violently overthrow the American government. Most blacks want simply a piece of the action. They just want to be in on the system. They simply want to enjoy some of this affluence.

And then we must take a look at that word "unrest." Most of the unrest in this country has not been committed by the Communists or instigated by them. It's been created by some very adverse circumstances and situations which have been produced, not by Communists, but again, by "God-fearing Americans." Many of the riots and disturbances that have taken place in many of our metropolitan cities were rooted in some oppressive situations — not because some Communists were marching through Harlem calling people to riot. These riots have grown up out of the police brutality, it's grown up out of political neglect, the unwillingness of the decision-makers in our society to listen to the cries and desperation of oppressed people. Indians are rising up on the reservations, not because Communists have gone up there, but simply because young Indians are sick and tired of being pushed around and kicked around and denied the right to have access to land in the country in which they originated. This is their country. They were here before the Europeans or the Africans or anyone else came. Chicanos are rising up because they are tired of being cheated and pushed into migrant work at almost no money for pay. And they're sick and tired of being exploited by an economic system simply because of their own ignorance of the economic system. That unrest is not created by Communists; it is unrest from injustice, unrest from pain, unrest from being stepped on. This is not to say there are not subversive activities and subversive groups in this country that would take advantage of tension in our midst. But they don't create it.

Why are we so divided as a nation?

THAT'S EASY. Because we have forgotten God. The Word of God says, "Blessed is the nation whose God is the Lord" (Ps. 33:12 KJV). The Bible also says, "Righteousness exalteth a nation: but sin is a reproach to any people" (Prov. 14:34 KJV). America has forgotten God, so it is divided economically, politically, racially, ecclesiastically.

BLACK POWER

What is black power?

IN 1966, DURING the James Meredith march in Mississippi, the term "black power" was heralded by Stokely Carmichael, and for a great number of people it ran chills up their spines. Black and white people didn't know what to think of it. To many, black power meant guerrillas running through the streets with machine guns ready to destroy and tear down the whole system. Others claimed it was a Communist conspiracy to take over the nation. Many of our right-wing friends said, "Young black radicals are going to get dressed in 'commie' uniforms and go down the street in tanks."

All kinds of attempts were made to define "black power." It met with resistance, even in the black community. To many conservative blacks, the people who heralded or used the term in their minds were the so-called radical fringe. But there were also many in the white community who heard that term and immediately knew there was nothing wrong with it, because any honest-thinking white person knows that if you live in a white community, you have white power. Go to any community in America: if the people of that community are white, then the stores in that community are run by whites, the banks are run by whites, the politicians are usually white ... because the people who live in that community tend to run the community. But the black community does not run itself. White society still runs the black community even though black people live there. Many white people understand that and know it is true. Many, however, also hate to think that black people who have been oppressed all these years would suddenly come to power and then use that power to reap vengeance on their oppressors.

And so the debates of black power continued to take place. President Nixon replaced the term with "black capitalism." We came up with all kinds of new titles and phrases for it, but the brothers who annunciated the term understood what they were saying and stuck with it — BLACK POWER!

Black power, therefore, could be defined as complete emancipation of black people from white oppression by whatever means black people deem necessary. The methods to achieve black power may include selective buying, marching, or open rebellion, but black power is essentially the freedom of black people to determine their own futures. Black power means black people will view themselves no longer as inferior, but rather with all the dignity God gave man as a crowning achievement of God's creation. Therefore, having the ability to carve out their own futures, in the words of Stokely Carmichael, "It is black folks taking care of black folks' business." And in the words of James Cone, "It is taking care of business on black people's terms and not on white people's terms."

Black power can also be said to be the political, economical, and social development of the black community by black people from a black frame of reference. For instance, black power can be an educational revolution in which black people seek to control the schools in their community. Essentially, in most black communities across America the educational systems are run by white people. It can be said that since black folk are not on white people's agenda, white folk are not capable of deciding what is educationally relevant to black people in that whites are not really concerned about the future of blacks. Thus if black people were allowed to make those decisions and policies which shape the educational future of their young people, the school systems would be more flexible and therefore more relevant to the needs of black students. Then the black student, when he graduated, would be more able to compete with the wider society, knowing who he is, accepting his blackness, and taking his experiences both in the black community and in the wider community to develop the needs of the black community.

Black Power

Next, black power is a cultural revolution in which black people are redefining themselves, hence rejecting the words "Negro" and "colored" for the word "black." "Negro" and "colored" are the white man's definitions and "black" is the black man's definition. It is a cultural revolution, because black people are redefining themselves and are serving notice on the wider society that if you want to deal with black folk, you must deal with them on their definition of themselves and not based on white people's conception of them.

Black power is also an economic revolution. Money circulates in the white community thirteen and a half times before it leaves the community. Money circulates in the black community only twice...meaning that when a black person has a job, he generally works for a white employer, collects his paycheck from that white employer, spends it in the black community where the stores are owned and operated by whites — who then take the money out of the community, thus keeping the black community depleted. The capitalist system is based on the profit motive. It is the profit that builds a community, meaning that the profits made in the community must remain there for hospitals, schools, and other essential services that are in the interest of the community's development. Since profits do not remain in the black community, these developments do not take place. Whenever a black person wants to apply for a loan to expand his business, he usually has to ask a white bank manager. Black people, thus, are always dependent upon the white society for their economic subsistence. They have always had to bend to the needs of the white, think the way the white society wants them to think, and live the way the white society wants them to live in order to get that money. As a result they are always living in a state of compromise, having to worry about what they will say and how they will say it so they won't offend the white people, to keep the money coming. Black power stands up and gives a resounding No to this kind of negativism and lack of self-affirmation.

Then also, black power is political power. It is black people electing the kind of black man who can represent the black community without being co-opted by the white society. Black power simply means black people being able to substantially depend upon themselves financially, educationally, culturally, and politically. When they build institutions within the community which are run by black people, who bend to the needs of black people, then black people will be operating from a position of power rather than from a position of weakness, able to deal with a wider society, eyeball to eyeball, rather than two levels down looking two levels up.

Slowly black people have begun to understand that in this country white people do not deal with themselves or with oppressed groups from a position of conscience, but rather from a position of power. For a long time, black people and all oppressed groups in this country worked on the assumption that white people or white society had a conscience. And simply by appealing to the morality of the white man's conscience, one could bleed from him the concessions needed to survive as a human being. But white society does not operate from a position of conscience; it operates from a position of power. Example: 1950 — "We will hold no discussions with Red China"; 1960 — "We will not have diplomatic relationships with Red China." And yet in 1970 through 1972, not only did we initiate diplomatic relationships, but for the first time we sent the President to China. That was because between 1950 and 1970 the Chinese fired off the atomic bomb and the hydrogen bomb. We know that they have the cobalt bomb and that they have missiles trained on some of our key cities. Now that China is operating from a position of power, we have to talk with them.

Black power essentially says, "Instead of integrating into a society that does not want us in the first place, we need to be about the business of developing the black community so that we can determine our own futures."

Do black people have more rights than white people do now?

I SUPPOSE by that question you mean, Are black people getting more opportunities than white people? The answer is No. It would seem that way because there has been so much discussion about the race problem in newspapers, magazine articles, and documentaries on television. A lot of people think, because over the last ten years so much discussion has been given to the injustice reaped against black people, that progress is being made. Others are drawing this conclusion due to the fact that some companies, to comply with the federal standards of having a certain percentage of black people working in their industry or plants, hired black people ahead of some white people. And many whites walked away saying black people were being given greater opportunities than white folk. This is not the case. The gap between black and white people economically is still a very wide one. In fact, the statistics show that in 1948 the average income separating white families from black families in the United States was $2,400 a year. Now in 1973, the average income that separated black families from white families was $4,800. So you can see that over the last twenty-five years the gap has not closed, but has widened economically. When you consider that, on the average, one person is working in the white family and two or more are working in the black, and the gap has widened — well, things are not closing up.

Many white people get disturbed when blacks are chosen in preference to whites in some places to compensate for injustices in the past or to make the situation more equitable in the present. But it is like having two children born at the same time. You take one child and lock him in a room; the only time you go into this room is to change his clothing and to feed and bathe him. Other than that, you allow him no social contact with either the rest of the family or the rest of society. You allow the other child to grow up normally. When both children reach the age of seven you decide you would like to bring the other child out and let him grow up with his brother. Of course, when you bring that child out you'll discover he doesn't know how to talk, he will probably be retarded in many ways...mentally, physically, and emotionally. He certainly won't be aware of the overwhelming social habits adopted in the family because he has never been exposed to them or allowed to grow up and develop them.

Now let's say you decide to take the retarded child, work with him in such a way that by the time both of them are twenty-one they will be emotionally, physically, and mentally on an equal basis. You're going to do this without retarding the progress of the child who was allowed to grow up in a normal way. Which child will you have to spend more time with? Which child would you have to give greater opportunities to? Naturally, you will have to give greater opportunities to the kid you shut out for seven years, in order to put him on an equal level with the kid who grew up normally — yet, providing the kind of opportunity for the normal child so as not to retard his progress.

You cannot take a group of people who have been shut out of a society's decision-making process for more than 350 years and then expect to make that situation equal. It doesn't matter whether you are talking about short term, intermediate, or even long-range plans, without some type of overcompensation in order to produce the more equitable situation. This over-compensation is not to go on permanently, but it is to go on long enough so as to create an atmosphere by which justice and equity can begin to prevail. No person has more rights than another. It's just that the society we live in thinks so and therefore provides more opportunity for some people. In this country, the United States of America, black people do not have more rights or more opportunities than white people. They just do not.

Do you agree with the methods used by the late Dr. Martin Luther King?

IT IS ALWAYS difficult to answer the question as to whether you agree with any man's methodology, because there will be some methods you will agree with and some methods you will disagree with. I think that for the context of history in which Martin Luther King came, his methods certainly were valid in the sense that he was one seeking to draw attention to the injustices in our society against black people. He did so in what he called a "militant nonviolent" approach, and through nonviolence he was able to point out the violent racism and oppression against black people. His method was to seek to unify black people in a determined effort to destroy racism and oppression in American society. To that extent I believe many of his methods were very valid. I believe some of them cannot be used today in order to be effective. I seriously question the validity of marches, pickets, and demonstrations in the 1970's. I think we are past that point, and I think the methods Dr. King used in the 1960's served their purpose. He got legislation passed, attention drawn to injustices in this country, and a great number of legislative and legal barriers have been broken down as a result of his methods. I think that today we must move in the area of enforcement of those laws and urge black people to take advantage of those laws for their own economical, political, and social development.

Do *you think Dr. King's philosophy will prevail and help the Negro attain his place in society?*

DR. KING'S philosophy is not the only philosophy that exists among black people. While it is the most popular, it is not the only one. You must realize that all philosophies — at least all methods that derive themselves from certain philosophies — prevail depending upon the conditions and the circumstances. I believe that in the period between 1955 and 1968 the philosophy of Martin Luther King was the philosophy we needed in this country, but I also believe we must move from that to different styles and different methods now, because the battles are no longer the same. We had great legislative battles to fight during those thirteen years — they have been won. We had great battles of confrontation to make America aware of the injustice in society — that we have done. We had to demonstrate — that we have done. But now we must move beyond that and out of each generation develop some new styles.

If you're concerned about the concept of violence versus nonviolence, that has never really been an issue. Violence and nonviolence are not philosophies but tactics. The tactics I must use depend upon my oppressor. The man who is stepping on me cannot tell me to be nonviolent, because if he continues to kick me and continues to step on me even after I have nonviolently asked him to get off my back, he is forcing me to violence in order to survive. I'm opposed to violence. I hope violence isn't necessary. I call on all people to restrain themselves. But I'm also realistic enough to know that the use of violence or nonviolence is not determined by the oppressed; it is determined by the oppressor.

I am a white teacher. What direction should I take with my black pupils? What opportunities does a white teacher have to lead black pupils to Jesus Christ?

FIRST, I BELIEVE that any white teacher who is going to teach black students, especially in the ghetto or in the inner city, will have to go through a "dehonkification" of his own mind. White teachers teaching in the black community, to be really helpful, will not simply be paternalistic or maintain the existing institution or social order that educationally oppresses black people; but he will have to go through a whole revolutionary process of learning how black people think. Learning their hurts. Learning how the education system in the black community is oppressing rather than developing black people. Working for the erection of new educational systems that will be relevant to the needs of black people — and I mean the abolishing of existing institutions and the erection of new ones that will be relevant to the black community. When I say "abolish," I'm not talking about tearing down the building or committing any acts of violence, but I mean doing away with the existing system and replacing it with one that communicates to and develops black students — one which gives them a viable educational experience. There are several suggestions, for instance, in the English class. When I was in school, I was taught that my ghetto dialect was bad; so I was made to feel ashamed of the way I spoke. What the English Department and what my English teacher should have said to me was that my ghetto dialect was good because it communicated: it communicated to the people on my street, it communicated to some of my relatives and friends. Therefore, since it communicated, it could not be bad. What they should have told me was that to succeed, to penetrate the wider society outside my community, I need to learn to speak a second language, namely, what is called "proper English." They should have told me that they wanted to help me be bilingual so I could function in both worlds, rather than make me feel inferior by telling me the language that I spoke was bad.

In music, teachers start off teaching black kids from the inner city Bach, Beethoven, Chopin. The kids haven't even learned to have a musical appreciation experience. One must start with the way these kids really are. It is not that they don't need to know Bach, Beethoven, and Chopin, but you begin where they are. Start with Aretha Franklin, Roberta Flack, Don Hathaway, Lou Rawls; lead them from the Jackson Five to Chopin, Stravinsky, and these other classical artists. Your opportunity to introduce kids to Jesus Christ can only come when you have identified yourself with their total need. I'm afraid there are many Christian teachers who want to teach in the ghetto solely for the purpose of giving black children a passport out of hell to heaven. While we are called to do this — and the Great Commission calls us to preach the Gospel — the gospel of Christ must be preached to the whole man, and if you are talking about "saving me" you must not only save my spirit, you must save my mind from ignorance, you must save my body from its shackles, you must save my emotions. Jesus Christ must deliver my total being. To introduce me to Christ and then leave me in poverty, hunger, and ignorance is to deny the truth of Jesus Christ who said, "I am come that they might have life, and that they might have it more abundantly" (John 10:10 KJV).

Scripture teaches that as a Christian I am on earth on my way to heaven. If I live out my normal life span and Jesus Christ does not return in the meantime, I will live until I am seventy or seventy-five years of age. During that time you must make sure that my body is sustained on my way to heaven. By preparing your students to live in the real world, not simply telling them that "Christ is the answer," but show them *how* Christ is the answer, you will be able to communicate Jesus

Black Power

Christ effectively as the central force that must be present in all men's lives to help them not only live in their environment, but change their environment and be the live models on earth of what's happening in heaven.

Your Christian witness must be directed not only to the black pupils in the school, but also to oppressive teachers in that school system — to oppressive administrators, to the people on the board of education who make decisions and enslave the minds of those black pupils.

Do you feel equality is obtainable in American society? If so, what does a white Anglo-Saxon Protestant Republican church have to do to breach the gap between white and black community?

IN THE FIRST place, I do not believe equality is something to be "obtainable." Equality is the God-given right of every human being. It is something which is rather to be realized than to be obtained, because the implication there is that those who feel superior always ask the inferior to struggle to obtain "equality," which means to live on the same level as his superior. The Bible already tells us that God has made us and that we are peers, already operating on the same level; it is just that we must become convinced of this in terms of our practices.

What the WASP (White Anglo-Saxon Protestant) church can do is cease to be White Anglo-Saxon Protestant Republican and begin truly to become a community made up of black people, Democrats, Socialists, Republicans, left-wingers and right-wingers. And all must abandon their particular political perspectives to begin to get God's perspective. It is unfortunate today that there are large numbers of Christians who honestly believe God has vested Himself in the Republican Party. I was amazed when, on CBS television sometime ago, a group of people who claim to be Jesus People announced they were aligning themselves with the Republican party on the grounds it most closely represented the principles of the kingdom of God. To me this is sheer nonsense and borders on blasphemy — to suggest that God has decided to settle down in one particular party when both parties have people who trust Jesus Christ and are seeking to bring about justice. Also, both parties are filled with tyrants and dictators. Therefore the Church must not stand on the left or the right, it must not be liberal or conservative, it must not represent a black perspective or a white perspective; it must represent God's perspective, it must address itself to the issues of our time.

I think a classic example of this kind of situation is when Joshua is mapping out the battle of Jericho. As he is doing so, he notices a man standing off to his side with an unsheathed sword and dressed in full military regalia. Joshua, upon inspecting the man, determines that whichever side he fights with will decide which way the battle will go. So Joshua approaches the man to check him out. Joshua asks him a few questions: "Who do you fight with? With them or with us?" The man gives him one No for both questions, saying, "It is as the Captain of the Lord's hosts I have come" (Josh. 5:14). To Joshua's question, "Do you fight with them or do you fight with us?" the answer was No! What the Lord was saying to Joshua was, "Joshua, I have not come to take sides; I have come to take over!"

What the church in America needs is to allow God, through Jesus Christ, to take over. This means Jesus Christ is neither Democrat or Republican, He is neither left-winger nor right-winger, He is neither American, British, French, African, Asian, Latin American, Canadian, nor what have you. He is neither capitalist, Communist, or socialist. Jesus Christ is Lord of heaven and earth and is come to build a whole new thing and to establish a whole new system. This system is built on Him, His priorities and values, and apart from Him there cannot be a new community.

Now, once we can start producing these kinds of new creations in Jesus Christ, we can build new communities that will bridge the gap between people, because then all the labels that we sport around will have been broken down.

BLACKS REACHING BLACKS

If you are a black Christian, do you need to become engaged in these methods and forms to fight racial discrimination in light of the fact that the Bible says, "In this world you will be persecuted and you will have tribulation"?

YES, THE BIBLE says I will have oppression, tribulation, and persecution because of my commitment to Jesus Christ. And I'm perfectly willing to be discriminated against, stepped on, and abused because of my commitment to the lordship and the authority of Jesus Christ. But I'm not willing to be abused and stepped on because I'm black.

How would you answer a black militant who says we serve a white man's religion?

A BLACK MAN does not have to be a militant simply because he believes Christianity is a white man's religion. We have got to stop this idea that just because a black person disagrees with our theological perspective, it makes him militant. He simply has a different point of view. Now, there are many blacks who do have their theology wrapped up in white cultural trappings. Any black person who is going to communicate Jesus Christ to another black person must make sure Jesus Christ lives within the confines of the black experience. There are many of us black people, like white people, who don't like the words "black theology" and the "black experience." But all theology is, is a study of God. Black theology is an attempt to find out God's view about questions being asked in the black community.

All theology should deal with God's point of view about questions constantly being asked. There's a different set of questions being asked in the black community than in the white community. The gospel of Jesus Christ must adapt itself to the black community, to the questions black people are raising. Many blacks who have been trained in white seminaries and white Bible schools and have gone through white theological academic studies tend to end up giving answers to questions that black people are not asking, scratching where black people don't itch. To that extent we do come across as being "white" in our theological and religious thinking. Once having overcome that, we can then begin to deal with any black person from the point of view of God Himself, who says, "look unto me, all the ends of the earth: for I am God, and there is none else" (Isa. 45:22 KJV). He is calling all the ends of the earth to look unto Him. John 3:16 says, "For God so loved the world that he gave his begotten Son, that whoever believes in him should not perish but have eternal life" (RSV). God commended His love toward us...all of us...that while we were yet sinners, Christ died (cf. Rom. 5:8).

What do you consider the most effective way to reach the black militants who are against institutionalized religion and the establishment?

I WOULD NOT want to reach black militants simply because they are against institutional religion and the establishment. I tend to be opposed to institutionalized religion. Any person who is committed to the authenticity of the Scriptures and any person who is committed to truth in general will

Blacks Reaching Blacks

have to recognize that institutional religion today is not where it's at. Certainly one must be very careful in defining the word "establishment," because the word is kicked around in many circles today without many people understanding what it really is. The establishment tends to be those people who are in control of our society. It is a fact that 1 percent of the population of the United States has 43 percent of all the cash; that 1 percent of the population of the United States has 39 percent of all the common stock invested in corporations; and that 1 percent of all the companies in America make 70 percent of all the profits. And these people within that 1 percent can be considered the establishment. The rest of us just work for them. Of course, one is not to be against the establishment simply because they are the establishment, but should be opposed to the evil they conduct, the iniquity they transmit. In terms of organized religion, it was never the will of God that the church become a super structure, but rather it was to be a movement of communities... people who can be identified with Jesus Christ, His life, death, and resurrection, and who by their commitment to Him and each other become the live models on earth of what's happening in heaven.

We must also be careful that we are not seeking to reach militants with the truth of Jesus Christ simply because they are black and simply because they are militant. Today almost anyone who stands up and speaks the truth is considered to be militant; almost anyone who opens his mouth against injustice today is a militant. The term "militant" has different definitions, depending on where you are or what political perspective you hold. If the word "militant" means to be aggressive, then surely even we who are followers of Jesus Christ should be considered militant. We are militant about justice; we are militant about truth; we are militant about mercy. I think the form militancy takes must become the issue. If we are talking about black militants who do not know Jesus Christ, that is one thing. I know a number of black militants who are thoroughly committed to the lordship and authority of Jesus Christ, who will differ from other black militants in the sense that while their goals might be the same in terms of liberation of black people, their methodology, their philosophy, and their frame of reference will certainly be different.

Now, in terms of communicating to those black militants who do not know Jesus Christ, reaching them must begin with identifying with those goals they have, which are commensurate with the kingdom of God. We must be able to show them that the message of Jesus Christ is socially relevant. It is relevant to the black man's struggle for liberation...to become the man God intended him to be. If the Gospel that we have to preach to them is only for the purpose of giving them a passport out of hell to heaven, then it will not be of relevance and they will be turned off.

Would you spell out just what Christians should do to reach black people with the Gospel? Are black Christians doing their part in this program?

PERHAPS THE MOST frequent question being asked by white Christians of evangelical persuasion today (in the United States) is just how do you communicate and reach black people? I must admit I am suspicious of that question, because I'm not so sure, even after telling white Christians what they can do, that they will do it. I think they are hoping I will tell them there is nothing they can do, so they will salve their consciences and continue to do nothing.

I think the first thing that can be done to reach black people is for white people to "dehonkify" their minds, that is, for white people to learn to "think black" and to understand the cultural thinking patterns of black people. I admit that there are black people who operate at different levels. I'm not talking about the bourgeois blacks who are essentially people with black skins and white minds; these are blacks whom you can relate to much easier. Many black people find that white people prefer to relate to those types of blacks; they can identify with them because essentially those black people are white people — they just happen to have black skins.

However, if one is talking about dealing with black people generally, then one is talking about dehonkifying the minds. White people have to learn to think black. It is unfortunate that in our society white people have not been given the opportunity to be multicultural. Black people have had that opportunity, and black people tend to be much more multicultural than white people, because we have been forced from school-age up to read Hemingway, F. Scott Fitzgerald, Shakespeare, and a host of other white authors and writers. To survive in the society and operate politically, economically, and sociologically I have to read the *New York Times* and the *Wall Street Journal* every day. I have to read *Newsweek, Time,* and *U.S. News and World Report* magazines every week. I have to read *Fortune* magazine once a month to be aware of what is happening in any segment of white society. But white folk are not obligated to read the literature of black folks. They are not obligated to read *Jet* and *Ebony*. Neither are they obligated to listen to the Soul radio stations out of which black music, black thinking, black dialogue, and black news develop. Thus white people in our society grow up culturally deprived. It is only at the point where white folk begin to deal with this cultural deprivation that you can ever hope to begin to communicate to black people; because, you see, people are emerging in this society where they are accepting their blackness and saying that if they are going to be accepted, they are going to be accepted on their black terms. Therefore white people who want to communicate to black people will have to communicate to black people on their terms, that is black terms.

Second, white people who want to communicate to black people the gospel of Jesus Christ must spend some serious time thinking through what the Gospel is and what its implications are. Unfortunately, most evangelicals are of the persuasion that the Gospel is offering to people a passport out of the physical hell fire into the glorious streets that are paved with gold and the gates of pearl that are swinging open wide, without seeing any real significance of the gospel of Jesus Christ to the kind of lives people must live from day to day. The message of Jesus Christ must deal with a man's need to eat. It must deal with his need to have a place to sleep. It must deal with his need to provide for his woman and his children. If the gospel of Jesus Christ does not deal with these basic facts, these basic necessities, these basic nitty-gritty affairs that men must live with, then the gospel message of Jesus Christ offers no real hope.

The third thing these whites — who have managed to de-honkify their minds and develop some schooling about what is happening in the black community and to think black — must do is to become missionaries to their own people. Their greatest need is not so much coming down to the black community to help "those dear colored folk" (although this is definitely a need), but rather, in terms of priority, is meeting the needs of their children, because the children are our future. If we get wiped out, we need to make sure the proper investment is being made so our children can develop in future generations.

When all is said and done, blacks have both less income and less wealth than whites. Even when adjustments are made for income differences, black wealth is only a fraction of the wealth of whites with comparable incomes. The income-wealth distribution with blacks is more unequal than with whites. Accumulated wealth of whites is influenced to a greater degree by interfamily transfers in the form of inheritance than is true for blacks. That is, in white society, money marries money. Very wealthy people do not marry outside their class. All you have to do is to check the majority of marriages of such families as the Mellons, the Vanderbilts, the Rockefellers, the Kennedys, Watsons, Sloanes, Motts to discover that this is true. So, much of the wealth white people accumulate is done through wealth marrying wealth as well as through inheritance. It is passed on from one generation to another and has little to do with pulling oneself up by the bootstraps.

Education, which is supposed to be the great equalizer, does not operate to provide the same income or wealth benefits to blacks that it bestows upon whites. That is, white people constantly say black people could advance themselves if they would only qualify themselves. But the overwhelming number of competent and well-trained blacks who are not receiving the same financial benefits for their education that whites do proves that education alone is not the answer for black people. It is only the most educated blacks, those with sixteen or more years of schooling, who are making any progress in closing the wealth-income ratio gap. The unhappy message of all this is that blacks are still a long way from achieving anything approaching economic equality. Blacks with superior education and skill do not reap the full fruits of their labors or endowments. The effect is to discourage younger blacks from acquiring the required educational skills in the numbers large enough and necessary to lift the entire income distribution of blacks, not merely that of what was formerly called the "Talented Ten."

W. E. DuBois, back in 1914, developed what was known as the "Talented Ten" theory when he argued that one out of every ten blacks would be talented enough to become the economic, political, and social leaders of the black community and thus pull the rest of the race up. The remedy to the economic plight, of course, is not to be found in economic activity alone. Until and unless blacks achieve some degree of effective political power — meaning command over institutions, public and private, which establish the rules of the game and determine the payoffs — blacks will continue to suffer from second-class economic citizenship. The purposes of almost any key black movement must serve as a challenge to weld together politically potent structures to create an environment in which black talent and aspirators might find opportunity for free expressions and uninhibited success. Without such structures, black economic development will continue to be just another black man's dream or, worse, a white man's cruel hoax.

I contend that the black church must become the new community that welds together these politically potent structures. According to data from the Equal Employment Opportunity Commission, blacks account for only 2 percent of the jobs at the top of the occupational ladder; it is at this end of the ladder that we find the decision-making echelon. One need only to pause for a moment to realize it is the nonblack decision-making process which selects, based on some criteria, one behavioral alternative from two or more possible alternatives. We are told what time to go to work, when to pick up the city's garbage, who will do the soldering, and so forth. More importantly, it is the nonblack decision-making process which decides that blacks will pay the taxes which will be used to pay nonblack farmers for not farming. Therefore the decision-making process is an important determinant in the struggle for economic power.

The goal to chart is clear: black people must get a grip on the decision-making process that controls jobs, housing, and education. First and foremost, blacks must recognize that the survival of black people depends on a sophisticated combination of political and economic action. This means strengthening the three supporting legs of a potentially successful strategy which includes black businessmen, black politicians, and the black community. The strategy involves corporative effort on both the local and national levels. On the local level blacks must gain effective access to city halls as they have in Newark, Cleveland, Gary, and other cities. Then black mayors will have access to the same public works budgets, the same insurance patronage, the same bank deposits as the Irish and Italian political machines. Then black paving and construction businesses will support Irish and Italian paving and construction business. Black businessmen and politicians must also be alert to the new opportunities they could develop. For example, now is the time to get on board at the front of the environmental gravy train. The time is now for modular housing construction. And now is the time for black politicians to see that black developers get a fair share of the public funds. Black people must devote more time and energy to such analysis, always seeking the economic and political strength of the nonblack politicians. Another strategy must be the pursuit of legislative tactics in which the nonblacks push legislation for financial help to Lockheed and other large businesses. Why not attach a rider to that legislation, calling for help for black businesses? There are many such special-interest bills of this type introduced in a given congressional term. We have to watch for them to use them to our advantage.

Can a man be a black militant and a Spirit-filled Christian at the same time? Is it right to assume that a black militant is one who wants action now and will go to any human means to accomplish change in the system?

WE WANT TO define our terms. When we talk about a militant, we are talking about someone who is aggressive, someone who is forward. We use that language even within religious circles when we speak of the "Church Militant"; we're talking about the church's being aggressive, being forward. Too many people in America, when they hear the word "militant," think of a person who has a machine gun in his hand, running through the streets prepared to shoot people down. Now, I am a "militant" — I'm militant about justice, I'm militant about mercy, about love. I'm forward and aggressive about those things. I'm not taking a machine gun and mowing anyone down. It is possible for a person to be black, to be militant, and to be Spirit-filled.

Our problem is, we assume that when a person becomes Spirit-filled [and by Spirit-filled we mean a person who claims Jesus Christ as Lord, because the Bible teaches that when

Christ is Lord of a person's life he is filled with the Holy Spirit] he must be docile, subjective, he is passive, allows people to kick him around, never raises his voice, never gets angry. But this is not true. Let's deal with the most Spirit-filled man who ever lived — Jesus Christ — and let's watch His behavior. In one instance He stands up and weeps over a city, cries over the injustice and inequity and immorality of the city. The same Spirit-filled man picks up cords and walks into a temple and cleans it out by whipping the moneychangers and stampeding the cattle out of the temple in a holy fury. This same Spirit-filled man looks at a prostitute and tells her her sins are forgiven; the same Spirit-filled man looks at the religious leaders of His day and calls them a "generation of vipers."

There are many moods, as you can see, to a person who is Spirit-filled. It is quite possible for a person to be Spirit-filled and organize a boycott against the supermarket in his neighborhood that is cheating people. It is quite possible for a person to be filled with the Holy Spirit and organize people politically to protect their rights in the community. It is quite possible for a person to be Spirit-filled and organize people to vote for certain candidates who might at least humanize to a certain degree the system that is oppressing them. In fact, I suggest to you that it would be far better to have Spirit-filled militants than to have people filled with the devil's intentions who are militant. The evil or the good does not lie in whether one is militant or nonmilitant; the good or the evil lies in whether one is filled with God's Spirit or not filled with God's Spirit. The question is, who is controlling the militancy? God, through the Holy Spirit? Or Satan, through his demonic forms? It is my prayer that there will be more militants raised up in our society today — people whose militancy is disciplined by the Word of God and the Holy Spirit.

Inherent in the question you are asking — when you talk of whether a black militant is one who wants to go to any human extremes to accomplish change in the system — is the assumption that all militants are the same. But you see, the struggle for liberation on the part of black people is being fought on many fronts. There are some fighting the battle in education, there are others fighting it in the entertainment world; others are fighting it in the political world; others fight it in the sports world; and there are also those fighting the battle in the ecclesiastical or religious structure. They all have different objectives or purposes in mind, so that all militants cannot be put into the same boat. There are people who are militant whose militancy is disciplined by their commitment to God and to His Word, and there are others who have other forms of discipline and frames of reference. They are all commonly engaged in the struggle for liberation. They will tend to disagree on some of the aspects of that liberation, and they will also tend to disagree in methodology — how it is to be attained. True, some will go to any means necessary, not only in death for themselves, but also in killing other people if they believe that is what will bring about liberation. There are others who believe there must be some way liberation can be secured without taking other people's lives. Some believe in no acts of violence at all, and others believe some form of violence is necessary. And so the battle goes, because there are different militants who have different perspectives. All militants, though, are committed to the fact that there must be some changes.

Now, I don't think any militant is naive enough to believe that the total society can be changed. But he might believe society can be humanized enough to get the oppressors off oppressed people's backs. And that is essentially all that black people are asking for. Black folk are simply telling white people, "Please get off of our backs and give us the right to determine our own futures." We're not necessarily asking you to rehaul the whole social fabric of your system, they say, but we are at least asking you to get off our backs, so that we can build a system we feel is suitable to live by. It may not be any better than yours, but at least it will be ours.

BLACK-WHITE RELATIONSHIPS

The black community today does not seem to be any longer interested in integration. Why not?

IF YOU REFER to my response to the question about black power you will understand some of the reasons. You must understand that black people moved away from integration because white people have essentially said they do not want it. Black people's historical struggle for integration never came about simply because they were that excited about becoming a part of the white society, but rather, at that particular time it was the only meaningful strategy blacks could adopt to survive in the kind of system we have in American society. For instance, when black people talked about integration in the school system, it was not that we were so interested in having our kids sit next to white kids but, because the system was run by white people, city councils and the state legislatures in various parts of our country made sure more money, more facilities, and better teachers were allocated to white schools. Many of us in the black community were struggling to get blackboards fixed, better laboratories for our students to study in, and more qualified teachers.

Knowing that white society always looks after itself, we saw clearly that the only way we could insure or guarantee quality education for our children was to have them sit in the same classroom with white people. But what we discovered was that integration, where it did occur and where white people did acquiesce to it, was always on white people's terms. Hence, whenever we discussed integration in American society we discussed black people going to white schools, black people moving into white neighborhoods, black people joining white churches, but we never talked about white people joining black churches or white folk moving into black neighborhoods or white people going to predominantly black institutions — because white people assume their institutions are superior. Thus we found integration meant the giving up of our culture and the negating of those institutions in our society that were not only historically but contemporarily meeting the needs of black people.

We discovered this was too great a price to pay for integration. We discovered we cannot have meaningful integration if a people are negating themselves, negating their culture, negating their history, and having no valid self-affirmation. We must understand that integration — or black power, for that matter — is not an end in itself, but rather strategy towards the liberation of an oppressed people. Integration is not a philosophy, black power is not a philosophy, but rather a strategy to meet the objective of a philosophy — which is the liberation of oppressed people.

What is the major hangup in black-white relations?

I BELIEVE there are two major hangups in black-white relations. One is ignorance — ignorance about culture and ignorance about history. Many people do not understand the history of racism in American society. It is on that score that I would suggest people get a copy of the book entitled *Before the Mayflower,* written by Lerone Bennett, published by Penguin Books, which is the first in-depth study of the development of the black community in America from 1619 to the present. Here you will be able to get an understanding of what created racism in the American society. You must understand the history of racism and the sin and evil in it before you can deal with it in the present. The other ignorance is cultural — the lack of understanding and appreciation of the respective cultures among black and white people. We don't seem to understand that cultures are not superior or inferior to each other — they are only different. In white people's culture, white people place little emphasis on one's sensuality, one's style. Therefore white people tend to smirk at black people because black people tend to condemn white people as lacking style, lacking feeling, lacking soul, lacking sensuality. What we must understand is that cultures are only different and that we both need each other to expand each other. It might be helpful to study the book *Black Rage* (published by Basic Books), which is written by Dr. Price Cobb and Dr. William Grier and is the first study of the psychic disorders created in black people by racism.

The second major hangup is sex. This is an area most white people don't like to admit publicly, but they do admit privately that their major hangup is sex. Any argument between two white people with a race question generally ends up with one saying to the other, "...And how would you like your daughter to marry 'one'?" Nothing is more devastating in the minds of the average white male than the thought that the day will come when he will have to compete with the black male for the hand of the same woman. Nothing is more disturbing in the white male's mind than the thought of sexual intercourse occurring between black and white people. Any number of times some white father who learns his daughter is dating a black male will in his rage say, "The thought of him having his dirty black hands over you!" Or in some instances it has been that when a white father has learned his daughter is dating a black male, he is looking for that black male with a gun to shoot him because it is a tragedy in the white man's mind that relationships could occur between a white woman and a black man.

Many white people suffer from the delusion that all black men are dying to have sexual intercourse with white women. Another myth existing among white people is that black people are sexually superior to white people. It becomes very difficult to explain to many whites that black folk come with the same standard equipment.

Many of these myths grew out of slavery. During slave days it was widely known that many slave masters spent more time with slave women than they did with their own wives, especially in white circles where white people tended to be very puritanical about sex, even within marriage. Any woman who enjoyed sex, or was expressive in her sexual relationships with her husband, was considered to be unladylike. So many of the fantasies that white males had, many of the things that they wanted to do sexually with their own wives but were afraid to, they found themselves able to do with slave women, because a slave woman had to submit. The more time the slave master spent with slave women the less time he spent with his wife, so this raised some suspicion in his own mind about what his wife might have been doing. This created within him the fear and insecurity concerning the black male. It was out of this fear that the white man during slave days created the concept of the "southern belle" — the untouchable white woman. And he began to make speeches like "We must protect the honor and the sanctity of our women." He began to put her on a pedestal. The more he put her on the pedestal, the more unreachable or untouchable she became to him — because the more you put someone on the pedestal, the more sanctified that person becomes, and nobody makes love to statues.

The white man's suspicion of the black man and his fear of him grew out of the system that white slave masters created — the stud system. This was where he forced a healthy black man to cohabit with a healthy female to bear healthy children. When the woman became pregnant, the man was moved to another quarters to do the same thing. Within the course of ten years this slave could have brought into the world a hundred children, but never be allowed to be father to any of them. It was out of this that white people would constantly gossip about and discuss the sexual powers of the black male. It also became rumor among white women who were not being sexually satisfied by their own men that they could find

Black-White Relationships

satisfaction with black people, because black females were sexually satisfied by their own men. They could find satisfaction with black people, because black males were sexually superior. Which of course is all a myth. There cannot be meaningful social relationships between black and white people in America until white people get over their sexual hangups about black folk.

I *am a Christian raised under segregation in the South. Is it wrong for me to have my children in a private school so they will not be influenced by the Black Panthers in the public schools?*

AT THE TIME of this writing, the Black Panther Party in America, for all intents and purposes, is a dead party. Black Panthers have never actually been that powerful. The Black Panther chapters have never numbered more than thirty. Yet they have been a potent movement in their confronting the black community with its need to come together to determine its own future. What made the Black Panther party sound so overwhelming was the tremendous amount of attention the news media gave it and the attempt on the part of many law enforcement agencies throughout the United States to try to destroy it legally.

By your question, you seem to suggest that the Black Panther Party is in control of the schools and that the best way to get your kids away from the Black Panthers is to send your kids to private schools. But the fact of the matter is that Black Panthers are not in control of any school, they are not in control of the black community and not even any small segment of it. Someone might be using the Black Panthers as a smoke screen to make sure that your children do not have to come into contact with black people at all. That would be like not allowing my kids to go to school where white people are, in order to keep them away from the Ku Klux Klan or the White Citizen's Councils.

Black Panthers may have only thirty chapters, but they are moving into many cities, even into schools in our area and are giving out their literature to the students there. Should our kids still be allowed to go?

AGAIN THE ANSWER, Yes. There are all kinds of people giving out literature to your children in school. Your kids are being given literature to take LSD; your kids used to be given literature not to go to school in the name of stopping the war; your kids are being given literature by the Ku Klux Klan or White Citizen's Council; your kids are being given literature by Jehovah's Witnesses and Catholics. Your kids get confronted with a whole lot of literature. The Black Panthers' literature is just one kind among much literature that your children will receive in the course of their student experiences, and in a number of cases he will have to make a choice to accept or reject. You cannot keep your kids separated from society, simply because there are elements in that society which confront your kids with ideologies that you don't like and maybe your children will not buy. Part of maturity in our time is to be able to say Yes or No.

What are the basic differences in principles and policies between the Black Nationalists and the Black Muslims?

BLACK NATIONALISTS advocate control by black people

of the black community. They believe black people ought to buy only from those stores owned by black people, ought to keep the money in the black community, and must pool their resources to develop the black community economically, politically, and educationally.

The Black Muslims believe the same thing with one exception. Their belief is based on some theological or religious dogma. The Black Muslims believe the white man is the devil; the spirit of the black race is God. And the Black Muslims believe the only way that this economic, political, and social control of the black community will ever develop is through the teaching of the Honorable Elijah Muhammad.

Essentially the philosophy of Black Nationalism and the philosophy of the Black Muslims are the same with the exception that the Black Muslims have a religious base from which to operate.

How can the Church help in the racial situation?

THE FIRST STEP has to be that the Church face up to the fact that there is a "racial situation." Many organized churches in American society have been happy simply to bury their heads in the sand like the proverbial ostrich and say there is no real problem. Or, there has been another group who've just been satisfied every time we bring up the racial situation to say, "Oh, Christ is the answer." Of course, these people tend to do that with all questions. If you tell them there is a pollution problem they say, "Christ is the answer." You tell them there is a political problem, and they say, "Christ is the answer." If you tell them there is war going on in the world, they say, "Christ is the answer." For those folk who are followers of Jesus Christ, the issue is not whether Christ is the answer — the issue is, What are the questions to which Christ is the answer? And the Church, especially the white churches in America, has refused to come to grips with what the problems are.

In order to help in the situation it must face up to what has produced racism in American society and to the nature of racism. One will discover that essentially the race problem in America is a white problem. You hear great numbers of people saying, "What can we do about the Negro problem?" — "the colored problem?" — "the black problem in America?" Well, black people didn't create racism, and black people didn't establish slavery. Black people didn't institute segregation, black people didn't lynch themselves, black people did not deny themselves access to jobs or employment and education. It's rather the white racist society that is doing that. Right away there will be people who say, "You can't generalize like that, there are some exceptions." Yes, but institutionally, governmentally, politically, and economically we live in a white racist society. Even government documents have made the statement, and I quote, "We live in two societies, separate and unequal" (the Kerner Report).

The second step the Church must take is to admit, confess, and repent of the fact that it, as an institution, has been one of the most grievous sinners in committing acts of racism. In fact, in many areas where so many other institutions were breaking down the barriers of segregation and racism, the white church in America continues to be the last bastion of resistance — so much so that over the years the Church, in many respects, gave divine theological credence to the institutional forms of oppression — slavery and racism. A large segment of the Church preached during the years of slavery that slavery was an institution ordained by God. They quoted the passage in the Bible (Gen. 9:20ff.) where Noah goes to bed drunk one night and his nakedness and drunkenness are discovered by his son Ham. The next morning when Noah finds out his son has mocked and cursed him, he then curses Ham's son Canaan. An ad hoc group of biblical scholars representing a certain wing of the Church has preached that since

Noah cursed Canaan, God also cursed Canaan, and they argue that Canaan was a descendant of Ham, and the word "Ham" was supposed to mean "black," and therefore God has cursed all black people and relegated them to the position of servitude.

When slavery became a way of life in American society in the seventeenth and eighteenth centuries, and millions of slaves began to be shipped here from Africa, thousands of them died along the way. Someone with a moral conscience raised the question, "Suppose they are not people?" or "Suppose the black man does not have a soul — suppose he is only part man?" During slave days the official theological interpretation of the black man was that he was part man. This led to constitutionally and legally declaring the black man to be only two-fifths of man. The Church must confess the fact that where segregation existed — for instance, in the school system — there the same people who sat on the board of education, the same people who were teachers, the same people who were principals of the school systems, were members of their churches. The same businessmen who were denying black people employment, refusing to promote them to management positions, refusing to allow them to gain full economic employment, were also members of their churches. The same political leaders who sat in the Congress and Senate and passed laws that further oppressed black people were also members of the Church. The Church must repent of this if it is going to help the racial situation.

Third, the Church must become a live model of what the kingdom of God is. The kingdom of God is made up of all people who have trusted Jesus Christ and who have been disciplined by Him. The Church can best help the situation by becoming live models, so that when oppressed people move through the country asking, "Where can we find justice?" the Church can stand up and say, "Over here! We practice justice." And when oppressed people go around asking, "Where can we find love?" the Church ought to be able to stand up and say, "Love is practiced here."

Fourth, to help this situation the Church must prophesy to

a racist society, a society that is entrenched in racism. In other words, the Church must be the voice of God against oppression. We must keep in mind that during the period between 1880 and 1925 more than eight thousand black people were lynched in this country without one white person ever being brought to trial for it. The Church remained strangely silent...and during all the periods of racial oppression in this country the Church has not opened its mouth. When the Church refuses to open its mouth, it is essentially saying that God hasn't anything to say, because the Church is the voice through whom God speaks. The Church must discipline those of its fellowship who put up their "For Sale" signs and move out of the neighborhood because it takes on a different racial tone. The Church must discipline those real estate agents in their churches who refuse to sell property to black people who can afford to live anywhere. The Church must discipline its members who are businessmen and educators who practice racism in the institutions they belong to. This is what the Church can do. The church congregation itself must stop moving out of its facilities as soon as the neighborhood changes, as it has done. The Church can become engaged in hitting the system where it really hurts — in its pocketbook — through economic boycott wherever institutions in our society fail to carry out the standards of a holy God in terms of racial issues. For instance, if General Motors is refusing to give black people equity within institutional corporate structure, then the Church, God's people, ought to covenant among themselves that they will not buy General Motors products. If A&P supermarkets are charging more for food in the black community than they are in the same kind of A&Ps in the white community; and if A&P refuses to promote black people to management positions in it — that is, to provide equality — then clearly God's people must get together and boycott A&P; and do the same with any other store or industry in American society that is practicing injustice against other members of the kingdom of God.

I am a white person, I was brought up with no race consciousness, I have always been accepted by others of all races. But lately I've found I am being automatically turned off by black people. How can I combat this?

FIRST OF ALL, you must accept for a fact that it has not been only lately that you have been turned off by black people. Black people have in significant numbers turned white people off for generations. It's just that white people didn't know that, because black people's survival was conditioned on giving white people the impression they were paying attention to them. It's only been lately that black people have begun to accept who they are and assert their manhood, and as a result they do not have to play games with white people any longer, but can begin telling it like it is and expressing their own true feelings.

It is unfortunate that, out of this, many black people are putting all white people in the same bag without first allowing the white person to prove himself innocent or guilty. On the other hand, you must accept the fact that you show some degree of naiveté when you say you have been raised in the United States of America with no race consciousness. That's almost impossible, unless you have been raised in a multicultural society where you are allowed to be free to mingle and to fellowship and to socialize with all kinds of people. Otherwise, it is almost impossible to be raised in America and not be a racist. I have been affected by racism in the American society, and the only difference between me and some other people is that I know it and am working on it. You can only combat this matter of black people tuning you out by beginning to understand and think "black."

Black-White Relationships   177

It is difficult for a white person, who does not understand what it means to be negated and stepped on and denied rights and privileges because one is black, to sympathize. I would suggest you do some strong reading in this area as a first attempt to school yourself as to what's happening to black people in America, so that you can effectively communicate with them. Communication, as I've said, is not so much what is being said as what is being heard. Many times white people say things that sound perfectly legitimate to them, but completely turn black people off because it means something else to black folk. An excellent book to get a hold of, that will give you some understanding of the history of back folk in America from 1690 to the present, is *Before The Mayflower* by Lerone Bennett (available in paperback from Penguin Books). The second book is *Black Rage*, by Price Cobbs and William Greer, which is the first in-depth study of the psychic disorders created in black people by racism. The third book would be the autobiography of Malcolm X, which gives you some understanding of perhaps one of the greatest heroes in the black community; it tells what it's like to grow up in the ghetto and all the difficulties that go with it. Some other books are *Black and Free*, which is the story of my background as a gang leader on the streets of Harlem; *How Black Is the Gospel*, which is my attempt to give some theological understanding of the context in which the message of Christ must be preached in the black community; *My Friend the Enemy*, by Bill Pannell, which will give you some understanding of the dynamics of being a black Christian in America; and *Black Power*, by Stokely Carmichael and Charles Hamilton, which will give you some understanding of the argument of the black-power advocates in this country.

ow can we explain to our children that it is all right to live with blacks, be integrated in schools and business, and yet not marry them?

YOU CAN'T. The moment you tell your kids that marrying blacks is out of the question, you are also telling them there is something wrong with mingling with them, being integrated with them in your social life and business. If you do not want your children to date and to marry blacks, the best thing to do is to keep them away from them. If your kids are going to grow up in the same neighborhood with blacks, play with blacks, go to school with blacks, have social life with blacks, date blacks, it will mean that some whites and some blacks intermarry. If you do not want that to take place, I suggest you keep them apart.

I'm glad you raised that question, because there are many white people under the illusion that black people are just dying to marry whites. But one must understand that in order for a marriage to occur, two people have to go down the aisle and both of them have to say, "I do." Many people seem to have the impression that blacks stand over whites with guns and knives, forcing them to marry them.

CRIME AND VIOLENCE

n view of your account of the activities in gangs and other reports we hear of danger in the ghettos, is it wrong to be afraid of these dangers? Should we go into or stay in these areas in spite of these dangers? What can we do to help in the ghetto?

ONE MUST NOT get the impression, simply because accounts are given of some antisocial behavior in some ghettos, that this is reflective of the entire ghetto. Unfortunately, when people read my own encounter as written in *Black and Free,* or the encounter of Nicky Cruz and Dave Wilkerson in *The Cross and the Switchblade,* or when they read Claude Brown's book, *Manchild in the Promised Land,* they get the impression these are indicative of the entire communities of Harlem or the South Side of Chicago, the West Side of Chicago, the East Side of St. Louis, the Watts District of Los Angeles, or the Hill District of Pittsburgh. This is not the case. Harlem and many other so-called ghettos in America have a strong middle class and a strong upper-middle class. A significant number of lawyers live in Harlem, school teachers, school administrators, authors, artists, musicians, as well as gang leaders and drug addicts. That simply makes Harlem identical to many, many other communities in America. There is a strong social life in the ghetto. Again using Harlem as an example, because that's where I've lived for most of my life, there is a strong cultural life there, a strong educational life there, and strong political activity. This social and cultural life could not exist if every inch and every block were infested with hoodlums killing people every two minutes.

Even if this were the case, my job and your job as Christians is that we are to be God's representatives everywhere He sends us. One function of God's people is to be a live model on earth of what's happening in heaven. Now, if you've got one million people living in Harlem, there must be some live models there of people who are committed to Jesus Christ, so we can't afford to run simply because there is danger. There must be live models on Indian reservations, and live models in Chicano and migrant areas. There must be live models in Beverly Hills and Westchester County as well as Harlem and Watts and many of these other areas. God's people are called to go into all the world...regardless of the danger. It seems stupid to sit down and talk about danger when we stand up in church and recite, "Yea, though I walk through the valley of the shadow of death, I will fear no evil: for thou art with me"...as long as it's not in Harlem...or Watts... or.... The Christian cannot concern himself about danger; he must be about the business of the Master.

I must admit that when white people ask, "What can we do to help in the ghetto?" I'm highly suspect of the question because I'm afraid that even after you tell them what they can do, they're not going to do it. There are some exceptions — thank God! But again it seems to be a simple matter of the Christian's discerning what the will of God is. The inaugural address of Jesus sums up what the Christian is supposed to be about anywhere. In Luke 4:18, Jesus says, "The Spirit of the Lord is upon me, because he has anointed me to preach good news to the poor..." (RSV). That good news to the poor is that God has come to tell them who they are in Jesus Christ, to help them stand on their own two feet and be, on earth, on the way to heaven, what God intended them to be. To get themselves together, redefine themselves in God's frame of reference and not in anybody else's. We are to help the blind to see — for except a man be born again, he cannot see. We must be in the ghetto to help people who are spiritually blind know what's going on.

"To bind up the brokenhearted." God knows that we who live in the ghettos are brokenhearted. We are broken from police brutality, dope addiction, oppression — economical, political, and social. Our school systems devastate us, not educating us within the reality of our experience. We're broken because our babies are bitten by rats. We are broken because we are forced to live in rundown, dilapidated, infested buildings while paying exorbitant rents. We are broken because when politicians make their political decisions they do not take us into consideration. We have no control over our own future. We're broken because beside all that social evil down on us, we are faced with the normal sin of all men — separated from Jesus.

What can we do? Bind up the brokenhearted. Preach good news to the poor. Help people who don't know the way to see. We're to preach release to the captives. We who live in ghettos are captives — physically, emotionally, mentally. All you have to do is read Price Cobb and William Grier's book *Black Rage* to see what racism has done to us emotionally and mentally. All you have to do is come to Harlem to see what it's doing to us physically.

What can we do to help in the ghetto? Simply do what Jesus tells us to do: "Bind up the brokenhearted, set at liberty those who are oppressed, preach the acceptable year of the Lord." That's what we can do.

There is a kid on drugs who is trying to find himself. How can we help him without turning him off?

PRIMARILY, BY NOT condemning his use of drugs — because his drug abuse is not his real problem. He is taking drugs as a substitute for something else. You must find out what his needs are, then begin to apply Jesus Christ to those needs. There are many Christians who simply assume that since Christ is the answer, there is no need to know what the questions are. The kid is taking drugs for numerous reasons.

You must find out first what his needs are, and then by the spirit of Christ you begin to meet his needs. Through meeting his needs, as well as by pointing him to the Liberator, Jesus Christ, his drug problem will incidentally be abolished. His drug problem is not his real problem.

What course of action do you feel the police should take in the midst of a riot?

I THINK THE question needs to be rephrased: "What course of action do you feel the police should take before a riot?" I assume you have in mind a riot in the black community, which obviously is slightly different from other kinds of riots. Many times the police in the black community are the cause of riots. One must understand the way the police conduct themselves in the black communities across America. They come across to black people as the occupational force in the black community for the purpose of maintaining the interest of white society. There are only two visible kinds of white people in the black community. One is, of course, the white businessman; ninety-seven percent of all businesses in the black community are white-owned and white-controlled. The other one is the police.

The problem with many white folk in America is that they assume the policemen as they know them in white suburbia are the same policemen in the black community. They don't understand that in the black community he puts on a different face. They also assume the police are very much the models of what we read when we were in the first grade in our "Dick, Jane, and Sally" books, where the policeman comes to help people cross the street, or help little old ladies obey the traffic lights, and generally in this kind and pleasant community one of these guys could build a fantastic relationship with the people. Unfortunately, this is not the case in a community like Harlem, the South and West Sides of Chicago, the Hill District of Pittsburgh, or Watts in Los Angeles. We must also keep in mind that many of us have lived in the South, where policemen were the enemy. Many policemen do not receive the kind of education that teaches how to operate in a multi-cultural society. Most of these policemen are lower-to-middle-class whites, with perhaps one year of education beyond high school on an average. They just do not know how to cope with the sociological and psychological problems of the black community. They do not understand the nature of the oppression of that particular community, thus they do not make good law enforcement agents. When a riot takes place, many of these policemen do not handle it from a legal point of view. They handle it emotionally, becoming emotionally hung up with name-calling, so all of a sudden they begin to bust heads out of a vendetta rather than acting toward keeping the peace.

The proof of this could lie in the difference in the way the National Guard or the federal troops responded to a riot around the Pentagon building in Washington, D.C., and the way the police responded to a riot in Chicago or Harlem. A kid goes up to a policeman and spits in his face, or goes up to a policeman and calls him names. The policeman immediately reacts by cracking the person over the head or by cracking several heads out of his emotional reaction. But the National Guardsmen were put in front of the building and given strict orders not to allow anyone to pass in front of a particular line. The National Guard's response to the crowd was, "Feel free, make as much noise as you'd like; throw as many bottles up into the air as you'd like; call me as many names as you'd like — just don't cross that line!" Therefore, you'd find that many of the National Guardsmen joked and talked with the demonstrators, with the young people. But the policemen, because of their philosophical attitude about what these young people are doing, tend to be much more emotional about their involvement than just keeping the peace.

A native New York white who lived there thirty-seven years ago says, "I used to live right near Harlem, and I could go down the streets and take my baby right into Harlem to go shopping. What has happened that a white person cannot go into Harlem today?"

THINGS HAVE NOT changed thirty-seven years later — white people not only go into Harlem, but white people also work and make their living in Harlem. There's always this groundless rumor that seems to circulate in many white communities (there are some exceptions) : "No white person can walk through Harlem and come out alive." No one mentions the fact that 75 percent of the police force in Harlem is white, that 60 percent of all the teachers who teach in Harlem are white, that 97 percent of all the storeowners and merchants in Harlem are white. These people work in Harlem all day and half the night and have managed for years to keep their heads on. This idea that black people are violent, that they are all switchblade, gun-carrying, violent anarchists and militants, is one of the greatest lies being perpetrated in America today.

Did you ever confess to the police the numerous crimes you committed as a gang leader? Why or why not?

AFTER MY CONVERSION I did go down to the local precinct and discuss with them my activities as a gang leader. I also went around the neighborhood, to stores I had raided, to people I had on occasions committed violence against, and I offered them opportunity to press charges against me. None of them did. I did so because I felt there needs not only to be repentance before God, but also repentance and restitution before men.

I *am a black student residing in the black community. Many of the fellows I grew up with are now addicts or junkies. I want to go back home to be able to relate and to help them. How do I tell them drugs are wrong without them putting me down?*

WE HAVE TO understand that the drug scene in the black community cannot be approached simply from its moral standpoint. Seeking to communicate to an addict that it is morally wrong for him to be taking drugs will not help him kick the habit. Rather, it must be first pointed out to the addict what drugs are doing to him physically. He has signed a slow death certificate; most drug addicts I've known didn't live past the age of forty. Drugs have also enslaved him spiritually, mentally, and emotionally. If he has become enslaved (and a large number of people in our community are on the drug kick), this means a large portion of the black community is emotionally, mentally, and spiritually enslaved.

It is conservatively estimated that in Harlem alone there are more than 50,000 drug addicts supporting a habit averaging more than $60 per person per day. No one can make that kind of money working each day in the black community. Therefore, many of these addicts have to become parasites on the rest of the black community in order to survive. And much of the so-called high crime rate in the black community can be directly attributable to the drug situation. Black people, already struggling to survive against an oppressive racist society, cannot afford the added luxury of having to fight parasites in their own community on such a large scale. We also have to communicate to the drug addict, besides his own personal enslavement, that the drug scene in the black community is also an attempt to negate the development of that community economically, culturally, politically, and educationally. One of the most effective methods the system has created to wipe out any revolutionary attempt on the part of the black community to get itself together has been the free distribution of drugs — not free economically, but free in the sense that the drug traffic goes unmolested by the so-called law enforcement agencies in the black community. The federal government, state government, and local city government refuse to bring all the resources of their law enforcement agencies to crack down, not only on the drug pushers within the community, but on those politicians and business people in high places who import the stuff and allow it to be distributed and sold, without fear of the law — and this is mere testimony of the system's commitment to continue to oppress poor and black people in this country. Remember that for years many of us who live in the black community have been working to get tough legislation passed to drive the drug pushers out — but there has been absolutely no motion.

Now, in recent times you've noticed a number of documentary films on drugs, a number of pamphlets, magazine articles, parent-teacher meetings with special guest lecturers, and there have been all kinds of special literature printed to parents on how to detect whether your child is on the "stuff." The reason for this great upsurge and interest in drug control in recent times is not because of poor people or black people being on it, but because the sons and daughters of the people who own the system have begun to experiment with drugs. When the sons and daughters of congressmen, senators, and governors go that route, then society becomes interested in cracking down on the drug situation. The people who own the system do not care about the deprivation and deterioration of the black community. It means those of us who live in the black community are going to have to take a stand against not only the drug addict, but against the pusher and against those law enforcement agents in our community who allow it to be circulated without the offenders being apprehended. If not, our community will perish.

It is a known fact that a drug addict can kick the drug habit within seventy-two hours through what is known as "cold turkey," or quick withdrawal. The real problem is that after he has gone through that stage of physically kicking the habit, he generally goes right back on the stuff because he cannot kick the psychological habit, or what he calls the "monkey on his back." Therefore, we must deliver him from his psychological, emotional, and mental hangups which caused him to have to depend on the drug scene in the first place. There must also be an opportunity to transform the community or to transform the individual. One's need at this point is for spiritual conversion.

I am not naive enough to state that only through Jesus Christ can a drug addict freely kick the habit, because Black Muslims and other groups who are not committed to the Jesus Christ of the Scriptures have managed to create converts in their midst who kicked the drug habit with no medical attention at all. But I do say that apart from some sort of spiritual crisis or spiritual conversion in a man's life, the drug habit cannot be kicked. I can say with intellectual integrity that while Jesus Christ is not the only person who can help an addict kick the drug habit, He is obviously a live option.

All right, Tom, suppose I go through this communication to a drug addict and tell him that taking drugs is an attempt to negate his manhood and to enslave his body, mind, and spirit, but he doesn't respond right away. Do I have to struggle with him through these changes?

YES, OF COURSE. This is one of the problems we face today. There are not enough persons around to help enslaved people struggle to their liberation. An addict has to go through physical hell in order to kick the habit, and he needs some one to stand with him in doing so. It's ludicrous to ask a fellow to kick the habit and then not be willing to be a brother to him and struggle with him through it. This holds true in many other areas, such as with prostitutes who need liberation. Are we prepared to struggle with the prostitute — to liberate her body from the pimp and the people who are buying her? How do we liberate the pimp from using our black sisters as property? How do we liberate our black men from abusing their women? How do we liberate our women from the negative attitudes about their men that have been created in them by the system? All this requires struggling. It requires people who are willing to love people and fall with them and cry with them and do all that is required to help them learn to be as free as God intended men and women to be.

This is one of the great issues the church has to struggle with. The church has become so institutionalized and so much of a social organization that it fails to recognize the imperative of Jesus that it be a community — and that it be a community of brothers and sisters committed to each other and committed to liberating other people. People are enslaved to many kinds of sin, but they are nevertheless enslaved. Even churches committed to some kind of a radical conversion make the mistake of expecting a person to stand on his own two feet and live a successful Christian life by himself once that person says he's converted. This is totally impossible. We need people. And if we don't have people to struggle with us, through our difficulties and problems, then many of us can't survive. God made us in such a way that we're social animals, and as social animals ...we need people.

Do *you think we, as Christians, should have weapons, such as a gun, in our homes to protect our home and family from those who might attack and destroy our property?*

I'M GOING TO answer the question the way you presented it. I would not lift a finger to attack another man who is attacking my property, because my property is one thing — attacking my family and my life is something else. I believe that if a man attempts to take my life or the life of my family, I must do everything possible — including an act of violence, if necessary — to stop him. The Bible tells me I'm the master and I'm the priest and I'm the shepherd of my home. If someone attacks my property, I'm not about to take another man's life because he wants to burn my house down; or because he wants to take some property that's insignificant. I'm not attached to any material goods here on earth, and I'm not about to risk my life or his for it.

There are too many Christians in our society who have adopted the materialistic point of view that property is more important than human life. Mayor Richard Daley of Chicago, and some mayors in other towns which have experienced riots and looting, issued statements, "Shoot the looters." In other words, a young man who picks up a $100 television set and starts running with it ought to be shot to death for $100. I can't see that in the name of God. If we are really anxious to shoot the looters, maybe we ought to make that resolution retroactive about 300 years and put the guns in the hands of Indians. There is no place in Holy Scripture that places property above human life. There is no place in Scripture that in principle calls us to be willing to die for property. The Christian is not attached to his property.

Crime and Violence   **193**

In the first place, there are many other people who quote Scripture which says, "Store up for yourselves treasures in heaven, where moth and rust do not destroy and where thieves do not break in and steal," and yet run around concerned about property values. It has also been one of the great racist tendencies among Christians in our society to be afraid to produce an integrated society on the grounds that it brings property values down when black people move into a community. Well, it seems to me that if you're committed to Jesus Christ and if your treasure is in heaven, whence you're looking for the return of Jesus Christ, you ought not to be too hung up on whether or not your property goes up or down.

I repeat, if it is necessary for me to use an act of violence to protect the lives of my family and other people, I am open to do that, and will do that. But I will not commit an act of violence or take someone else's life simply to protect a piece of property. My commitment to Jesus Christ calls me to have responsibility to my family. It also calls me to some sort of responsibility to the man who is attacking my property...trying to steal it. It also calls me to some type of responsibility to the man who attempts to take my life.

BLACK OPPORTUNITY

he American system offers free education to everyone. Why, then, do so many black people drop out of school? Is it not true that through education, depression and poverty will meet its downfall?

THE ANSWER TO your latter question is No. Education does not destroy poverty. You must keep in mind that much of the schooling in American society is not really education, but indoctrination. And we send most people to school, black or white, for the purpose of getting an education to get a better job, to make more money. Education is provided in our society to learn to make a living, but no one ever teaches people through education how to live.

The reasons for numerous black people dropping out of school are many and varied. One, of course, is the common one: white kids and black kids drop out of school because they're bored, because they don't see what education will do for them down the road. Some of them are just plain lazy and don't want to follow through. But other blacks drop out of school because of the irrelevancy of the school system to the kind of environment and situation they grow up in. What good is it to be motivated toward education when you already know the system is not going to allow you to do anything with it. If you are going to motivate a student toward education, you must show him what good it's going to do for him. We have not done this for a great number of black, especially black-urban, people.

A second reason is, the education system in American society is run by middle and upper middle class people who have established middle and upper middle class values. Here is a black youth from an urban or rural area whose value system

Black Opportunity   197

from his home has been completely different; he arrives in the classroom, he is given white people's standards, white people's methodology of education for which he has no background, and it takes him two or three years to begin to adjust to that system. Each year he is being put further and further behind because he cannot psychologically adopt the cultural mores of a white society. He is given a first grade reader about Dick, Jane, and Sally and a dog named Spot who says Bow Wow. Dick is white, Jane is white, and Sally is white, and Spot is the exception — they integrated him. But the pupil is not like Dick, Jane, and Sally. Dick, Jane, and Sally live in the suburbs. Dick, Jane, and Sally have a swimming pool in the backyard. They swing from trees and they jump rope and they play and they go on trips and vacations with their parents. Well, this young man in the ghetto might not have both his parents, certainly he has no swimming pool in the backyard, and there are no trees and hardly any grass (of the green type) in his neighborhood.

The majority of the teachers in the school system who are teaching the boy are white and don't really understand what it means to be black or understand black thought processes. The principal of the school is white, the people who draw up the educational curriculum are white, the people who discipline him are white, and thus all this pressure makes the educational system irrelevant. The only way he can survive in the school system is to learn to think white, which means he has to negate his blackness.

There *are* blacks who succeed in the school system because they are prepared to compromise their blackness and to adopt white thought processes and to adopt the cultural mores of the white society. But there are others who cannot make that adjustment, and will *not* make it. There are the few who will adapt themselves to the white cultural mores for the purpose of receiving an education and not give up their blackness, but they are rare indeed.

Many school systems in America still have, and function off of, the I.Q. system. In the past all students were given the I.Q.

test, which for many years parents, teachers, and educators had deluded themselves into believing was a test of the intelligence of the student, when all the I.Q. test actually did was test the student's social awareness. The I.Q. test was made up — again — by white people with middle and upper class cultural mores. This black kid — who comes from a society which has no relationship to white society, from a black community where he might lack both parents, who has not been given the advantages of reading and other things that white students would have at home even before they start kindergarten or the first grade — sits down to take this I.Q. test. He scores a 96 on it. A 96 says he's an idiot. Now, the kid is not an idiot — he just doesn't recognize the forms. He's not aware of the symbols of the society that made up the I.Q. test. The teacher, looking at his I.Q. score, says, "This kid is an idiot." Therefore, he can't learn, the teacher decides, and this teacher tends to respond to the student as if he's an idiot, and the student responds by acting like an idiot.

To prove this point, a group of black psychologists got together and created what was known as a "chittlins" test. This was an I.Q. test made up by black psychologists, using black symbols known in the black community. They gave this I.Q. test to thousands of white, middle class, suburban kids all over the country, and the majority of these kids scored in the idiot class. That didn't mean these white kids were idiots. It meant they were not aware — emotionally aware — of black symbolism, any more than a black kid would be totally aware of white symbols. These are some of the factors that cause black students to drop out of school.

One other thing would be attitude in the classroom. A test was conducted by some experimentalists who took a litter of rats or guinea pigs, brought in a private, independent research group, and they said, "Here's what we would like you to do. We have breeded one group of these mice for intelligence. The other group of mice are normal, dull mice. We would like you tell us how much more superior in intelligence the smart rats are from the dull rats." The independent research group spent several weeks researching, studying, and experimenting with the mice. Finally they came back and told this group that the intelligent mice were five times more intelligent than the dull ones. And the original group looked at them and laughed. They said, "You see, the truth of the matter is that all these mice were the same. All of them were breeded the same. None of them had been treated any differently. We just told you one was superior to the other one, and because you believed us, you treated one group as if they were superior. They responded as if they were superior because you treated them that way."

This is true in the educational system. If a teacher walks into the classroom and believes a kid is an idiot, and gives that impression, why should the kid want to continue to go to school? There is no question that there is much talk today about the communication gap which exists between black and white, young and old, parents and children, college administrators and students, etc. Where do we start to solve some of these problems and bridge these gaps? Well, I think the key is the word "communication." Someone said, "Communication is not so much what is being said, but what is being heard." The tragedy we face in the twentieth century is that we don't communicate very well; we don't hear each other.

We talk today about people who want to affect change needing to go through normal channels, etc., but even when people go through normal channels they don't get a hearing. People sit down and calmly tell us where they're hurting, and we don't listen. It's only when they start making noise, jumping up and down and even burning something down, that we stop to take notice of what they are saying. And it's because we have a communication gap. I don't think it's so much a gap between young and old, or between administration and students, or between parents and children, as it is that we don't know each other and we tend to deal with each other based on our positions and not with each other as hurting people. And so parents deal with their children like stereotyped children, children deal with their parents like stereotyped parents; college administrators deal with students like stereotyped students. We don't look at each other as people.

The best way to start bridging the gap is for us to sit down, not as parents and children or as students and administrators, but to begin to sit down as people... people who are hurting, people who have problems, people who are trying to find their way. We must admit our common problems. By admitting our common wounds and hurts we begin to forge community among ourselves and can move on from that point — because we now trust each other, we all know that we hurt in the same places, and we won't use our positions to intimidate or usurp each other, but rather to aid and develop one another. Students are suspicious of administrators because they think administrators only want to use their positions to oppress students. An administrator in a student's mind is not really committed to the needs, interests, objectives of students. Administrators, on the other hand, think kids are a bunch of rebellious anarchists — stupid young people who have no sense of value about the "good old days." Parents are always telling their kids about the way it was when they were kids, and the kids are trying to tell parents about the way it is now. Kids think their parents are a bunch of old fuddy-duddies; parents think their kids are a bunch of young, snotty upstarts who can't be told anything. They all tend to view each other from perspectives that have to do with their positions rather than to sit down and deal with each other as people who are hurting, and to recognize the various goals, responsibilities, and objectives each one has.

One reason why Jesus Christ has established a new community to be called the Church is it was His desire that the church become the catalyst for this kind of meeting... where we come and meet each other as creatures of God who are hurting, in need of redemption and healing, in need of reconciliation. I think sometimes that if we didn't wait until a crisis developed, but got to know one another in less crucial times, we could therefore respond to each other more positively in times of crisis. I think, for instance, that if people in labor and the people in management spent more time just sitting down getting to know each other as persons, spending more time hurting with each other and baring themselves emotionally to each other, they would be far more amiable when it came to negotiations with their respective constituencies. I believe that if the students and faculty got to know each other or a more social basis, outside the academic halls and outside the scholastic institutions of higher learning, this would solve many of the problems that exist between administrators and students, between faculty and students.

Do you believe our government's welfare program is helping people realize who they are and realize their goals in the ghetto?

THE WELFARE SYSTEM in America is a classic example of governmental incompetence. The objective is right — to seek to take disadvantaged people who do not have opportunity and who are physically handicapped, to make sure they are provided a living. This I believe any society should do, and it's both moral and biblical.

But in many communities, especially in the large urban centers, many of the people on welfare are forced to have it at a tremendous cost. For instance, the father must be absent from the home for the mother to collect welfare. This breaks up the home, forces the man to leave home for his family to eat. Now, there are some very naive people who would say, "Well, then, why doesn't the man go out and get a job?" You see, they're looking at that from a white man's perspective. They don't seem to understand that in our society there are numerous black males who cannot find work purely on the grounds that they are black. But they also cannot find work because the society in which we live created a school system that did not quality them to work in the present technological age in which we live. Many people on welfare in large urban centers are subjected to all kinds of harassment by social workers and welfare supervisors who snoop on them to make sure that the woman is not sleeping with a man, no man in the house, and all this kind of stuff. This is tremendously damaging to the children who must grow up without a father image because of the present welfare system.

There are also many people who will point to the abuses of the welfare system on the part of the people who are on welfare. And you always read about the cases where some mother is receiving four or five different checks and making as much as $1,000 a month. Yet all the statistics prove that a very small percentage of people are living that kind of life, and simply because a few people are abusing the welfare system does not mean it is not valid to take care of the poor. I think, also, our society must understand that if there are poor, disenfranchised, unemployed people, it's a sickness within the society as well as a sickness and a handicap to the people going through it. Therefore we must find a way to create a system that takes care of the handicapped, and also takes care of the disenfranchised, while properly preparing them to move to gain full employment, in which a person can decide his own future and stand on his own two feet.

Another thing is most people who talk about welfare don't understand that the majority of the people on welfare in this country are white, and the majority of the people who abuse the welfare system in this country are white. They also overlook the fact that the majority of the people on welfare don't want to be on welfare. People in urban centers as well as in rural areas are asking for opportunity, not handouts. But when we fail to provide them with the opportunity, we've got to see that they are provided for by some other means or forms, such as welfare.

It's also very strange that American white society has a different word for welfare, depending on the kind of supplementation the government is giving. The majority of middle and lower income people who own houses in American society in the last decade have done so through what are called F.H.A. loans (Federal Housing Administration loans). These loans are a form of welfare—the only problem is that we don't call that "welfare," we call it "subsidizing." And so you see, when you're black you're on welfare, but when you're white you're being subsidized. The railroads in this country have received welfare; the airlines have received welfare; a lot of industries in America get welfare. More than fifteen golf country clubs in this country have built fabulous golf courses to the tune of well over $25 million, through loans supplied by the Department of Agriculture of the United States. Is that not welfare—welfare to play golf? Think of the number of automobile, General Electric, or telephone workers who have been out on strike over the past few years who, as soon as they have gone on strike, have applied for welfare checks. The taxpayers have been paying able-bodied persons who had jobs and who quit those jobs to go on welfare. Is it right to support people who have jobs and have quit their jobs because they are striking and then not be able to take care of people who can't have work?

I*s there any country in the world where the black man has more opportunity than here in our own country?*

THE ANSWER is yes. In East Africa, Kenya, Uganda, and Tanzania black people run the government, black people run the schools, black people are beginning to run most industries, but at least black people are making the decisions that determine their future. There are places in Africa, or in the Caribbean islands such as Jamaica, Barbados, Trinidad, or other nations where black people are in control of their own countries, where they have greater opportunity than black people do here.

Now if you mean "opportunity" to be material possession, there is no nation that has the standard of living the United States has. Someone has pointed out that black people in America own more refrigerators and Cadillacs than all Africans put together. But to me the ownership of refrigerators and Cadillacs is not "opportunity."

By "opportunity" I want the right to develop to my fullest potential, and I want the right to determine my own future. It doesn't make any difference how much money or how many refrigerators or Cadillacs I have, how many electronic gadgets I have in my house. The unfortunate thing is that white people in America continue to define opportunity as the ability to accumulate material possessions; when blacks talk about opportunity, we mean the right to develop to our fullest potential of what God intended us to be, and the right to control our own future, to control those institutions that maintain power over us. The logical question following that question is this: if there are greater opportunities in other places, such as Africa, then why don't black people go back to Africa or go to Barbados or Jamaica or Trinidad? Simple. My forefathers shed their blood, died. My black great-grandparents, grandparents, and parents fought, died, and shed their blood for the right of black people to own land and determine their own future in this country. I'm not about to forfeit their sacrifice by going back to Africa or any other nation.

You *stated that oppressed people don't have opportunity. What about Michigan State University and its Negro president?*

WHITE PEOPLE down through the centuries have always been able to point to one or two successful black people as an indication the system isn't all that bad. You can be assured that when a black man becomes president of an institution like Michigan State University or is selected to the board of General Motors or gets appointed to the President's Cabinet, black people rejoice. You also know that the politics of the United States has many times made single black appointments simply as token efforts to make sure that the situation is kept cool. I'm not suggesting this is the case at Michigan State — it is not. The man there happens to be one of the most qualified men in perhaps all of the United States, black or white, to be president of that institution. We are simply suggesting, though, that the appointment of a president here and a vice-president of something there is not the total answer to the problem. The answer will not come until black people have their share of power and positions throughout the United States. We make up 10 percent of the population of America. It is only when we become representative that way in television, in the news media, when that proportion controls the athletic field, controls that proportion of the wealth and political influence in this country, etc., that we can then say the country is making progress.

In the early part of 1969 or late 1968 a man by the name of James Forman presented a document known as the "Black Manifesto," in which he demanded $500 million in "reparations" for black people from the mainline denominational churches. Will any of this go to present Jesus Christ? What do you think about black reparations?

SUPPOSE YOU HAD two children, both of them born on the same day, and you decided to take one child and lock him up in a room and not expose him to anybody and go into that room only to bathe and clean him, change his diapers, and feed him when he needed it; you provided no social contact for that child. You allowed the other child to grow up normally until he was seven years of age. When he's seven years old, you would like the child who has been locked up to come out and be able to grow up normally as his brother did. You know, of course, when you bring the child out that he might not know how to walk. He certainly will not know how to talk. There will be a certain amount of mental and physical retardation in that child.

Let's say now that you decide with both of them at seven years of age that by the time they are twenty-one, they should be equal in terms of intelligence, knowledge, physical build, etc., without retarding the progress of the kid who grew up normally. You know you would have to spend more time, more effort, more money, more energy, have more patience, and take more pains with the kid whom you locked up than with the kid who grew up normally. To a great extent, to bring the child who is steadily locked up, or locked out, to equal status with the child who was normal, you will have to exercise some form of reparations with that child. This is true in race relations. Black people have been locked out of the system. They have been legally locked out through active conspiracy on the part of government agencies, churches, and other institutions over the past 350 years.

Now that the society has come around to deciding that, at least, they ought to consider no longer being that exclusive, they must also recognize that there must be a certain amount of reparations to make things just, to allow black people an opportunity to catch up, to determine their own futures.

I don't necessarily agree with the program of reparation as established by Mr. Forman several years ago. Mr. Forman presupposed that because he conceived the idea of reparation, he also had all the intelligence and the ability, or at least he and his group did, to decide what was good for black people and how that $500 million dollars was to be spent. I don't think any one person can decide that in the black community. But I do believe there are forms of reparation that ought to be considered. I believe those colleges and universities which have locked black people out of their educational institutions these many centuries ought to begin to provide scholarships for black people, to make up for it so that we can prepare black people, without financial strain, to become the leaders and technicians and administrators and developers of the black community.

I believe there ought to be considerable sums of money invested by ecclesiastical and religious groups in the development of black theological learning, so that we can prepare young men and women to become pastors, teachers, and spiritual developers and leaders in the black community, operating on a black premise of dealing with the problems of black people from a theological perspective that is black. I believe industry in American society ought to be promoting black people — be training, qualifying, and promoting numerous black people to management positions — to make up for the loss of access to the decision-making process in our society. I honestly believe that for a period of time, when there are two people competing for the same job of equal qualifications — one black and one white — the black ought to get the job, simply because of the need for reparation. This ought not to go on forever, but for a period of time in order to produce equity and more balance in the society.

The problem with many white people is, they want to produce equity without making the sacrifice that must be made to attain it. You have to realize that if for 350 years you've had all the advantages and black people have had all the disadvantages, white people will have to suffer some disadvantages in order to rectify the situation.

You ask whether any of the money James Forman was trying to raise in the name of black reparation would go to represent Christ. Probably not in the sense you understand it, because James Forman wouldn't know what you mean when you talk about representing Christ. What he is committed to and interested in is liberation and the ability of black people to determine their own futures. The people who are making these decisions include Christians and non-Christians. One must understand that not everything we do in our society has the Christian basis for it in the first place. There are many persons among us who want to preserve the American system, not because it has anything to do with God, but because it's got to do with our livelihoods. And there are black people who think the same way. They want the black community to develop because of their economic and social welfare and not necessarily because of the presentation evangelically of the message of Christ as you and I understand it.

You also must understand that many black people who talk about presenting Christ do not see it in the same way that many white evangelical conservative Christians see it. Presenting Christ would mean the verbal presentation of Christ and His claims; presenting Christ can also mean being a live model through which He is living one's life; presenting Christ can also mean being engaged in the destruction of the works of the devil; being engaged in obtaining justice, healing the sick, helping the blind to recover their sight, putting clothes on naked people's backs, feeding hungry children. All these things are also the works of Jesus Christ. There are many black people who become more committed to the outworking of the Christian message than to its theological and intellectual implications. You see, white people spend a lot of time arguing about whether a thing is conservative or liberal, whether it's modernistic or fundamental. Black people have never been engaged in those kinds of hangups.

While I disagree with Mr. Forman's methodology in reparations, I agree in principle that the idea and concept of reparation is biblical, it's godly, it's righteous.

PERSONAL ROLES IN SOCIETY

hy is it that we do not see more black women participating in the Women's Lib Movement?

THE ANSWER is that black women have already been liberated. You must consider that for one hundred years or more the black woman has carried the burden of helping the black race to survive. Looking back to slavery, we see that the slave system did not allow marriages to occur. On most plantations they had what was known as the stud system. This was where a healthy male was forced to cohabit with a healthy female; when the woman became pregnant, the male was moved to other quarters to impregnate other women. Very few children went around the plantation saying "Mommy" or "Daddy," because they didn't know who they were. Where marriages did occur, a slave master performed them temporarily by saying, "You promise to stay together until death or distance do you part" — the distance meaning every year at the slave auction, when the mother would be sold in one direction, the father in another, and the children in another.

When emancipation came, the discrimination that followed was directly against the male. He was not allowed an education. He was denied the chance to develop his own future. He was denied economic opportunity or employment. But the woman was allowed to work because she was less threatening to the white male ego. She carried the burden of being the breadwinner, which put the man out in the street because his manhood suffered from sitting at home watching his woman carry the burden and not being able to provide a living for his family. During this time the white woman sat at home while the white man went out and earned a living. In fact, a white man would take great pride in being able to work and say his wife did not have to work; as a result he also was the decision-maker in the society. White women have recently risen up and declared that they want to be decision-makers. So now they want to leave home and go out and compete with their husbands, whereas the black woman is saying, "I have already been out there competing with the white man. I want to go home and take care of my children and send my man out to compete with the white man." That is the reason why you do not see black women in the Women's Lib Movement.

The survival of any race is conditioned upon the survival of its male. The black community has always placed its emphasis on development of the black female. For instance, in times past if a family had two children and could afford to educate only one, generally the girl got the education. This was done because the woman who did not have an education had to work in surroundings where she could be easily exploited sexually by the white males in those surroundings. If she was educated, she could work in professional surroundings and pretty well control her own future. The man was considered able to find a way to make it somehow. Therefore women emerged the more educated in the race. They were given the more professional jobs, and even today more than 65 prcent of all that are considered professional white-collar jobs in the black community are held by black women.

A study of the Jewish community in the United States shows a completely opposite picture. Jewish women went out and broke their backs working to supply funds to educate their husbands so that the man could emerge as the leader of the community and the leader of the family. The system's attempt to destroy the black community has always been through attempting to castrate and destroy the black male. That is the reason why black women cannot afford to be caught up in a Women's Lib Movement. That would force them into competition with their men. Rather, black women must work now side by side with their men. In fact, some black women are committed — when they hold positions in government, or business, or industry — to having to deliberately make an effort to develop the black male. Some women are committed to working themselves out of a job so a black male can replace them. They consider it that crucial to the development of the race.

A close look at the black church shows that black women predominate in the leadership of the black church. After the pastor, generally the people who make the church move are the black women. The black church has failed immeasurably in the development of the strong black layman.

What should be a Christian attitude towards homosexuality?

IT IS INTERESTING that you should ask that question because my experience is that most church people want to avoid dealing with the question. It's the kind of question talked about in dark spots or under the table, but never openly. The best attitude we can have is one of understanding. It is only as we understand the problem of homosexuality that we can begin to deal with it. We must also admit that there are various extremes in dealing with it. Some churchmen openly advocate allowing homosexuals to be married by the church and allowing them into fellowship in the church. Others believe homosexuals ought to be totally disbarred and nothing done with them at all. A study of the Scriptures helps us to understand that homosexuality is not God's norm for sexual relationships. In other words, "there is a better way."

No one is born a homosexual. Homosexuality is developed as a result of one's environment and conditions that bear upon an individual psychologically. Let me give you an example of one social situation which leads to homosexuality. Quite often where a young man is raised in an environmental situation where women predominate, it can lead to homosexuality. There are many young men in the country who grow up without their father. Therefore, they are raised by their mothers

The Sexual Revolution   215

or some other female. If the woman is a very strong, aggressive, domineering type she will be able to control him without a man. But she might control him to his detriment, so he might grow up to be a "momma's boy" or a homosexual. He will relate aggressiveness and domination with a female and not with a male. He will, therefore, picture the woman as a disciplinarian, as an aggressor. He will picture a woman as a person who seeks to dominate him and will turn to men for affection, attention, and love — which will manifest itself in sexual practices as he gets older.

Another example is where a young man is raised in the kind of environment that carries very strict mores and values about sex. In fact, he is taught mainly that sex is dirty, that it is no good, that men who want sex are dirty and evil. So in order not to be evil or dirty he abates his normal sexual desire. Nobody tells him that having sex with another man is dirty and so, in an attempt not to appear dirty, he negates the normal sexual relationship with a woman and seeks to find outlet for his desire with a man.

Many women turn to homosexual (lesbian) activity — some, for instance, as a result of bad experiences with a man. There are many women who, because of very tough experiences with their fathers, their boyfriends, or even with their husbands, later in life will adopt an attitude that all men are no good, men are beasts, men don't understand — and they end up crying on the shoulder of another woman who supplies an outlet for them. Or a woman has a very bad sexual experience with a man. Many women have never experienced sexual orgasm with their husbands and can say honestly that in all the years they were married, they never had a climax. In discussing this with other women, they find there are women who are willing to help them reach that climax through homosexual experience. It is very strange that our society is much more tolerant of women who are homosexuals than they are of men. It is against these kinds of backgrounds that the church must seek from a biblical base to deal with the problem of homosexuality.

To simply say that Christ is the answer and all one has to do is accept Jesus Christ as Savior and homosexuality will go away is naive. Some homosexuality is the result of congenital hormone imbalance. Many women who have received Jesus Christ as their Savior have never had a sexual orgasm with their husbands and cannot honestly say that they enjoy sexual relations with their husbands. There are many men who have received Jesus Christ into their lives who are inadequate lovers to their wives. There are many men who have committed their lives to Jesus Christ who are still impotent. For instance, I know many Christian girls who have been told all their lives that sex is dirty, men are no good, and all that men are interested in is sex. Stay away from sex, it is dirty. Of course, the mothers told them this in an attempt to keep their daughters virgins until they were married, but in so doing left them with a very negative attitude toward sex. Then one of these girls reaches twenty-four years of age, becomes engaged, gets married, and on the day of her wedding the mother slips into her room while she is putting on her wedding gown and says to her daughter, "It's okay now." And this girl is expected in a matter of hours to wipe out all the negative attitudes she has been given about sex — which she can't. Her sexual relationship with her husband, both on their honeymoon night and throughout their marriage, becomes a disaster unless the husband is a very delicate and sophisticated teacher as well as lover.

Because many of these women cannot shake many of these attitudes given to them about sex in their earlier life, they have very bad experiences with their husbands and often turn to homosexuality for release. Simply telling that girl that all she has to do is accept Jesus Christ as her personal Savior in order to change her negative attitude about sex, is also wrong. She has to be taught. And if the church is going to deal with the problem of homosexuality as well as the other sexual hang-ups among the people of God, it will need to establish in its teaching program the godly attitudes about sex which should be taught. We could receive input from any number of Christian professional people on this subject.

What do you think about interracial adoption, that is, black people adopting white children, or white people adopting black children?

INTERRACIAL ADOPTION can be one of the greatest instruments of creating understanding for future generations. I say that with some qualifications and reservations. These qualifications and reservations would put black parents at a distinct advantage simply because of the fact that in order to survive in the society, black people have always had to know and understand white people. White people's survival is not based on understanding black folk. It is quite possible that a black kid raised in a white neighborhood would not know, eventually, how to relate at all to black people. Therefore those white parents must be careful that their children grow up and live in a multiracial society. This is also true for black parents, although it is inevitable that the average black family will have more contact with the white world than vice versa.

For instance, black students in order to get through school must study white history. They must study English literature written by white authors. To survive as a businessman a black man has to read *Newsweek, Time, U.S. News and World Report, Wall Street Journal,* and *Business Week.* He has to watch and listen to the news, which chiefly tells what's happening in the white world. Few white people are forced to read black history, listen to black music, study black poets. Few white people, to get through school, have to read *Ebony* or any of the black news periodicals. Thus black people are much more acclimated to the white world than are white people to the black world.

If white people adopting black children are sophisticated

enough to live in a multicultural society, to expose their children to all kinds of people, and to be bridge-builders, interracial adoption could add a tremendous dimension of life to the parents as well as to the society.